Samsung Galaxy Tab 4 for SENIORS

Studio Visual Steps

Samsung Galaxy Tab 4 for SENIORS

Get started quickly with this user-friendly tablet

www.visualsteps.com

This book has been written using the Visual Steps™ method.
Cover design by Studio Willemien Haagsma bNO

© 2014 Visual Steps
Author: Studio Visual Steps

First printing: August 2014
ISBN 978 90 5905 240 6

Resources used: A number of definitions and explanations of computer terminology are taken over from the *Samsung Galaxy Tab User Guide.*

Do you have any questions or suggestions?
E-mail: info@visualsteps.com

Would you like more information?
www.visualsteps.com

Website for this book:
www.visualsteps.com/samsungtab4
Here you can register your book.

Subscribe to the free Visual Steps Newsletter:
www.visualsteps.com/newsletter

Table of Contents

Foreword

Dear readers,

The Samsung Galaxy Tabs are user-friendly, portable multimedia devices that offer a wide range of possibilities. They are suitable for many different purposes. For instance, sending and receiving email messages, surfing the Internet, taking notes, planning a trip, or keeping a calendar.
The Samsung Galaxy Tabs come equipped with a large number of standards apps (programs) that you can use for instance, to work with photos, videos and music. You can also easily share your photos with others.

Apart from that, you can search the *Play Store* for many more free and paid apps. What about games, puzzles, newspapers, magazines, fitness exercises, and photo editing apps? You can find apps for almost any purpose you can think of.

In this book you will learn to use the main options and functions of this versatile tablet.

We hope you have a lot of fun learning how to work with the Samsung Galaxy Tab!

Studio Visual Steps

PS
We welcome your comments and suggestions regarding this book.
Our email address is: mail@visualsteps.com

Introduction to Visual Steps™

The Visual Steps handbooks and manuals are the best instructional materials available for learning how to work with mobile devices, computers and software applications. Nowhere else will you find better support to help you get started with *Windows*, *Mac OS*, an iPad or other tablet, an iPhone, the Internet or various software applications such as *Picasa*.

Properties of the Visual Steps books:
- **Comprehensible contents**
  Addresses the needs of the beginner or intermediate user for a manual written in simple, straight-forward English.
- **Clear structure**
  Precise, easy to follow instructions. The material is broken down into small enough segments to allow for easy absorption.
- **Screen shots of every step**
  Quickly compare what you see on your screen with the screen shots in the book. Pointers and tips guide you when new windows, screens or alert boxes are opened so you always know what to do next.
- **Get started right away**
  All you have to do is have your tablet or computer and your book at hand. Sit somewhere comfortable, begin reading and perform the operations as indicated on your own device.
- **Layout**
  The text is printed in a large size font and is clearly legible.

In short, I believe these manuals will be excellent guides for you.

Dr. H. van der Meij
Faculty of Applied Education, Department of Instructional Technology, University of Twente, the Netherlands

Visual Steps Newsletter

All Visual Steps books follow the same methodology: clear and concise step-by-step instructions with screen shots to demonstrate each task.
A complete list of all our books can be found on our website **www.visualsteps.com**
You can also sign up to receive our **free Visual Steps Newsletter**.
In this Newsletter you will receive periodic information by email regarding:
- the latest titles and previously released books;
- special offers, supplemental chapters, tips and free informative booklets.

Also, our Newsletter subscribers may download any of the documents listed on the web page **www.visualsteps.com/info_downloads**
When you subscribe to our Newsletter you can be assured that we will never use your email address for any purpose other than sending you the information as previously described. We will not share this address with any third-party. Each Newsletter also contains a one-click link to unsubscribe.

What You Will Need

To be able to work through this book, you will need a number of things:

A Samsung Galaxy Tab 4, TabPro or NotePro
Do you own a newer Samsung Galaxy Tab? This book may also suitable for your Tab. Please check the web page that accompanies this book for more information:
www.visualsteps.com/samsungtab4
The screen shots in this book have been made with a Tab 4. If you own a TabPro or a NotePro, some tasks are performed in a slightly different way. These differences will be explained in the relevant sections.

A computer or laptop with the *Samsung Kies 3* program installed. In *section 1.8 Downloading and Installing Samsung Kies 3* you can read how to install *Samsung Kies 3*.
If you do not own a computer or laptop, perhaps you can use a computer owned by a friend or family member to perform certain tasks such as upgrading firmware.

For the printing exercises you will need to have a printer manufactured by Samsung. If you do not own a Samsung printer you can just skip the printing exercises.

The Website Accompanying This Book

On the website that accompanies this book, **www.visualsteps.com/samsungtab4**, you will find more information about the book. This website will also keep you informed of changes you need to know as a user of the book. Be sure to visit our website **www.visualsteps.com** from time to time to read about new books and gather other useful information.

How to Use This Book

This book has been written using the Visual Steps™ method. The method is simple: you put the book next to your Samsung Galaxy Tab and perform each task step by step, directly on your device. With the clear instructions and the multitude of screen shots, you will always know exactly what to do next. By working through all the tasks in each chapter, you will gain a full understanding of your Samsung Galaxy Tab. You can also skip a chapter and go to one that suits your needs.

In this Visual Steps™ book, you will see various icons. This is what they mean:

Techniques
These icons indicate an action to be carried out:

 The index finger indicates you need to do something on the Tab's screen, for instance, tap something or type a text.

The keyboard icon means you should type something on the keyboard of your Samsung Galaxy Tab or your computer.

The mouse icon means you need to do something with the mouse on your computer.

The hand icon means you should do something else, for example rotate the Tab or turn it off. It can also point to a task previously learned.

In some areas of this book additional icons indicate warnings or helpful hints. These help you to avoid making mistakes and alert you when a decision needs to be made.

Help
These icons indicate that extra help is available:

 The arrow icon warns you about something.

 The bandage icon will help you if something has gone wrong.

1 Have you forgotten how to do something? The number next to the footsteps tells you where to look it up at the end of the book in the appendix *How Do I Do That Again?*

In separate boxes you will find general information or tips concerning the Tab.

Extra information
Information boxes are denoted by these icons:

 The book icon gives you extra background information that you can read at your convenience. This extra information is not necessary for working through the book.

 The light bulb icon indicates an extra tip for using the Samsung Galaxy Tab.

Test Your Knowledge

After you have worked through a Visual Steps book, you can test your knowledge online, on the **www.ccforseniors.com** website. By answering a number of multiple choice questions you will be able to test your knowledge of the Samsung Galaxy Tab. If you pass the test, you can also receive a free *Computer Certificate* by email. Participating in the test is **free of charge**. The computer certificate website is a free service from Visual Steps.

For Teachers

The Visual Steps books have been written as self-study guides for individual use. They are also well suited for use in a group or classroom setting. For this purpose, some of our books come with a free teacher's manual. You can download the available teacher's manuals and additional materials from the website: **www.visualsteps.com/instructor**

The Screen Shots

The screen shots in this book indicate which button, icon, file or hyperlink you need to click on your computer or Samsung Galaxy Tab screen. In the instruction text (in **bold** letters) you will see a small image of the item you need to click. The black line will point you to the right place on your screen.

The small screen shots that are printed in this book are not meant to be completely legible all the time. This is not necessary, as you will see these images on your own Samsung Galaxy Tab screen, in real size and fully legible.

Here you see an example of an instruction text and a screen shot of the item you need to click. The black line indicates where to find this item on your own screen:

Sometimes the screen shot shows only a portion of a window. Here is an example:

We would like to emphasize that we **do not intend you** to read the information in all of the screen shots in this book. Always use the screen shots in combination with the display on your Samsung Galaxy Tab screen.

1. The Samsung Galaxy Tab

The Samsung Galaxy Tab is an easy-to-use tablet made by Samsung which will enable you to do many things. Not only can you surf the Internet and send emails, you can also keep a calendar, play games, take pictures, shoot videos and read books, papers or magazines. All these things are done by using *apps*. Apps are the programs installed on the Samsung Galaxy Tab. Along with the standard apps that are already installed on your tablet; you can add many (free and paid) apps by using the *Play Store*. This is the web shop where you can acquire new apps.

If you connect your Samsung Galaxy Tab to the computer you can use the free *Samsung Kies 3* program to manage the content of your tablet. After you have safely disconnected the tablet from the computer, you can use the tablet anywhere you want. Depending on the type of tablet you have purchased, you can connect to the Internet through a wireless network (Wi-Fi), or through a mobile data network.

In this chapter you will become acquainted with the Samsung Galaxy Tab and you will learn the basic operations for using the tablet and the onscreen keyboard.

In this chapter you will learn how to:

- turn on or unlock the Samsung Galaxy Tab;
- set up the Samsung Galaxy Tab;
- use the main components of the Samsung Galaxy Tab;
- perform basic operations on the Samsung Galaxy Tab;
- work with the onscreen keyboard;
- update the Samsung Galaxy Tab;
- connect to the Internet through a wireless network (Wi-Fi);
- connect to the Internet through a mobile data network;
- download and install *Samsung Kies 3*;
- connect the Samsung Galaxy Tab to the computer;
- safely disconnect the Samsung Galaxy Tab;
- create a *Google* account;
- register your *Google* account on your tablet;
- lock or turn off the Samsung Galaxy Tab.

1.1 Turning On or Unlocking the Samsung Galaxy Tab

The Samsung Galaxy Tab may be turned off or locked. If your Tab is turned off, you can turn it on like this:

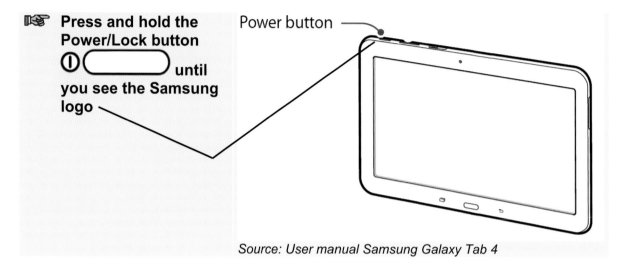

Source: User manual Samsung Galaxy Tab 4

The Tab is turned on.

Your Tab may be locked. The screen will be dark and does not react to touch gestures. If this is the case, you can unlock the Tab like this:

☞ **Briefly press the Power/Lock button** ⓘ⎯⎯⎯⎯⎯⎯

You may still need to unlock the screen as well:

☞ **Place your fingers somewhere on the right-hand side of the screen**

☞ **Drag across the right-hand side of the screen**

If this is the first time you turn on the Samsung Galaxy Tab, you will see a few screens where you can enter various settings. In the next section you can read how to do this. If you have previously used your Samsung Galaxy Tab, you can continue with *section 1.3 The Main Components of the Samsung Galaxy Tab* on page 23.

1.2 Setting Up the Samsung Galaxy Tab

You can set the language for the Samsung Galaxy Tab:

If English (United States) has already been selected:

☞ **Tap** Start ❯

If another language has been selected:

☞ **Tap the language**

☞ **Tap**
English (United States)

☞ **Tap** Next ❯

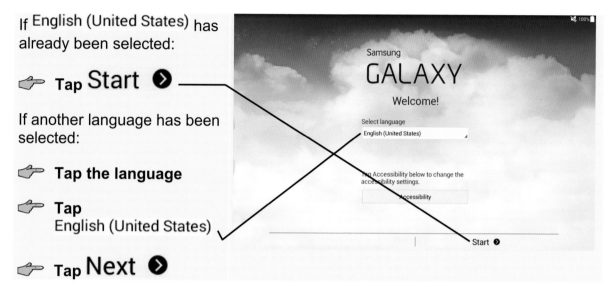

On the next screen you may see a message regarding a SIM card:

☞ **If necessary, tap** Skip ❯

On the next screen you can set up a Wi-Fi connection. You can skip this step for now:

At the bottom of the window:

☞ **Tap** Next ❯

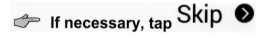

Now you can set the date and time:

If the time zone and the time are not yet correct:

☞ **Tap**
Select time zone
GMT+00:00, GMT

Date and time

Set date
21/05/2014

Set time
3:13 PM

Select time zone
GMT-04:00, Eastern Daylight Time

☞ **Drag upwards across the screen until you see your time zone**

☞ **Tap your time zone, for example**
Eastern Time
GMT-5:00

Now the time zone is correct and you will see the correct time on your screen:

☞ **Tap** Next ➤

In the next screen you will be asked to agree to the licensing agreement, and whether you want to send any error log messages in case the update procedure on the Tab does not work:

☞ **Tap a checkmark** ✓ **by**
I understand and agree

☞ **If necessary, tap the**

radio button ⬤ **by**
Yes

☞ **Tap** Next ➤

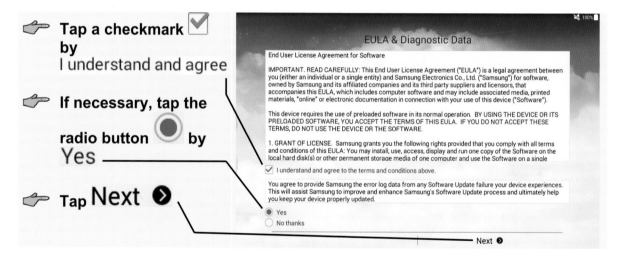

You may see a screen where you are asked if you already have a *Google* account. Many *Google* and *Android* functions require a *Google* account. A *Google* account is a combination of an email address and a password. Since you need a Wi-Fi connection or a connection through a mobile data network in order to sign in or create an account, you can skip this step for the time being:

☞ **Tap**

In the next screen you can set up a *Google* account. For now you can skip this step:

 **Tap**

In the next screen you will be asked whether you want to use the *Google location services*. This service uses information from a Wi-Fi or mobile data network to determine your location, even when you are not using your tablet. This information is used to enhance *Google* search results, among other things.

If you wish, you can uncheck the boxes:

☞ **If you wish, tap the boxes** ✅ ─────

When you see ☐ the option is not active anymore.

☞ **Tap** **Next** ➋ ─────

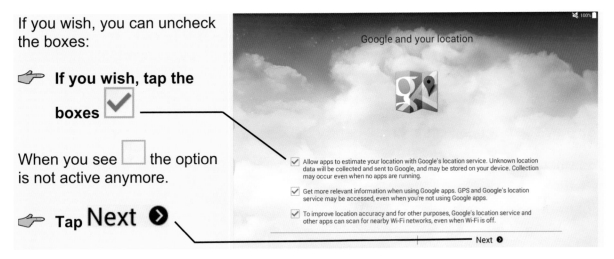

In the screen that is displayed you can enter the name of the tablet's owner:

Type your first name, if you wish ─────

☞ **Tap** ▶

Type your last name, if you wish ─────

☞ **Tap** ▶

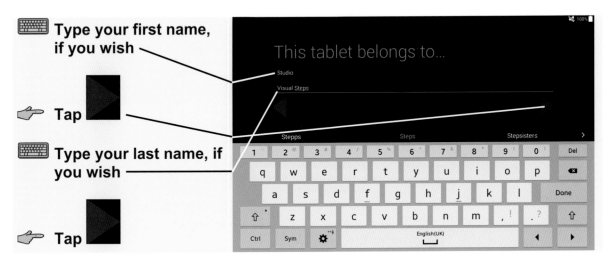

In the next screen you can set up a Samsung account. You can skip this step for the time being:

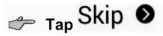 **Tap** **Skip** ➋

You will see one more screen, regarding the *Dropbox* storage service. You can skip this screen:

☞ Tap **Skip** ❯

Now the device is set up and ready for use:

☞ Tap **Finish** ❯

➥ **Please note:**

While you are using your Tab you may see some screens that provide information about the operation of an app or the keyboard. You can read the information and tap

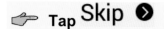

afterwards.

You may see a window on the right-hand side. This window will disappear by itself:

You will see the home screen:

 HELP! My Samsung Galaxy Tab is locked.

If you do not use the Samsung Galaxy Tab for a while, it will automatically lock. The default setting for locking is after 30 seconds of inactivity. This is how you unlock the Samsung Galaxy Tab:

☞ **Briefly press the Power/Lock button**

☞ **Place your fingers somewhere on the screen**

☞ **Drag across the screen**

1.3 The Main Components of the Samsung Galaxy Tab

In the images below you see the main components of the Samsung Galaxy Tab. When an operation regarding a specific component is described, you can return here to find the relevant component in these images.

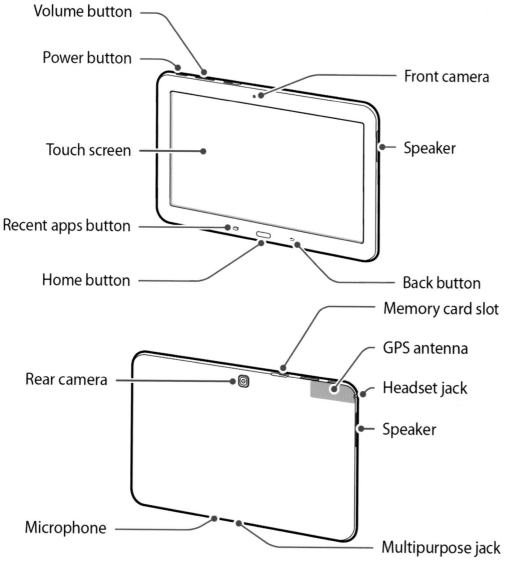

Source: User manual Samsung Galaxy Tab 4

On the TabPro and the NotePro, the memory card slot can be found on the right-hand side. On the NotePro, the multipurpose jack is also located on the right-hand side.

On the home screen you will immediately notice the large rectangular panels. The Tab 4 has two of these panels, whereas the TabPro has only one panel. These panels are actually *widgets,* small applications that provide information and useful functions:

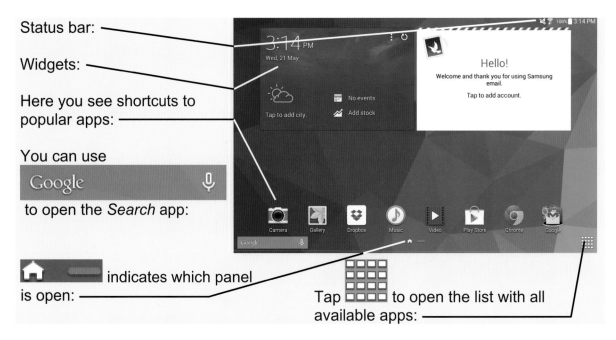

Status bar:

Widgets:

Here you see shortcuts to popular apps:

You can use

to open the *Search* app:

indicates which panel is open:

Tap to open the list with all available apps:

At the top of the screen you see the status bar. The current time is displayed on the status bar. To the left of the time indicator, you will see small icons that provide information regarding the status of the Tab and its connections. Below you see a list of possible icons that you may see and what they indicate:

Battery charging.

Battery level.

The Samsung Galaxy Tab is connected to the computer, but cannot be charged. For instance, because the USB port does not provide sufficient energy.

Indicates that the Samsung Galaxy Tab is connected to a Wi-Fi network. The more bars you see, the stronger the signal.

There are open wireless networks (Wi-Fi) available.

No signal.

No SIM card detected (in a Samsung Galaxy Tab suited for Wi-Fi and mobile data networks).

Indicates that the Samsung Galaxy Tab with Wi-Fi + 3G/4G is not connected to a mobile data network.

Indicates that your provider's 3G or 4G network (on the Samsung Galaxy Tab Wi-Fi + 3G/4G) is available and that you can connect to the Internet through 3G or 4G.

Indicates that your provider's EDGE network (on the Samsung Galaxy Tab Wi-Fi + 3G/4G models) is available and that you can connect to the Internet through EDGE.

Indicates that your provider's GPRS network (on the Samsung Galaxy Tab Wi-Fi + 3G/4G models) is available and that you can connect to the Internet through GPRS.

Active call (on Samsung Galaxy Tab Wi-Fi + 3G/4G models).

Call waiting (on Samsung Galaxy Tab Wi-Fi + 3G/4G models).

Missed call (on Samsung Galaxy Tab Wi-Fi + 3G/4G models).

Call forwarding has been activated (on Samsung Galaxy Tab Wi-Fi + 3G/4G models).

Smart stay has been enabled.

Bluetooth has been enabled.

Airplane mode has been enabled. When your Samsung Galaxy Tab is in this mode, you will not have Internet access, and you will not be able to use any Bluetooth devices. Nor will you be able to make any calls or send text messages, if you have a Samsung Galaxy Tab Wi-Fi + 3G/4G model.

Music playback.

Warning: an error has occurred, or you need to be cautious.

Connected to the computer.

Message notification. This may indicate that an update is available, for example.

Screen print has been made.

Alarm is set.

Notification for an appointment.

New email message received.

New text message received.

New *Gmail* message received.

Busy downloading data.

Busy uploading data.

Synchronizing.

GPS data are being received.

Options for opening the onscreen keyboard.

1.4 Basic Operations on a Samsung Galaxy Tab

The Samsung Galaxy Tab is very easy to use. In this section you will be practicing some basic operations and touch gestures:

☞ **If necessary, briefly press the Power/Lock button**

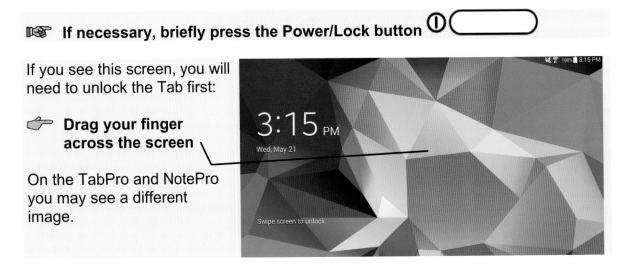

If you see this screen, you will need to unlock the Tab first:

☞ **Drag your finger across the screen**

On the TabPro and NotePro you may see a different image.

Now you see the home screen. Although you have set the date and time with the set up, the date and time may not be correct. You can easily adjust these settings. First, you open the *Notification Panel*:

☞ **Drag your finger downwards, starting at the top of the screen**

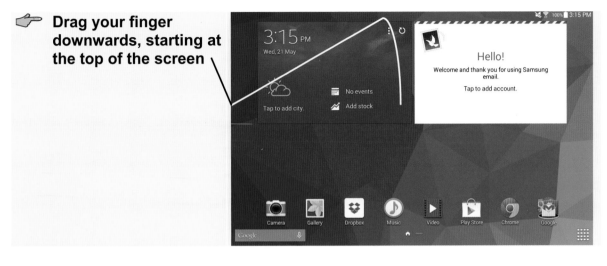

You will see the *Notification Panel.* In this window you can view messages concerning the status of the Samsung Galaxy Tab, and you can change a few settings. In the *Settings* app you can change many more settings:

☞ **Tap ⚙**

You will see the *Settings* app:

You will be using this app regularly to change all sorts of settings on your tablet.

To open the general section:

☞ **Tap**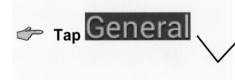

☞ **Tap**

🔲 Date and time

☞ **Tap** Set date

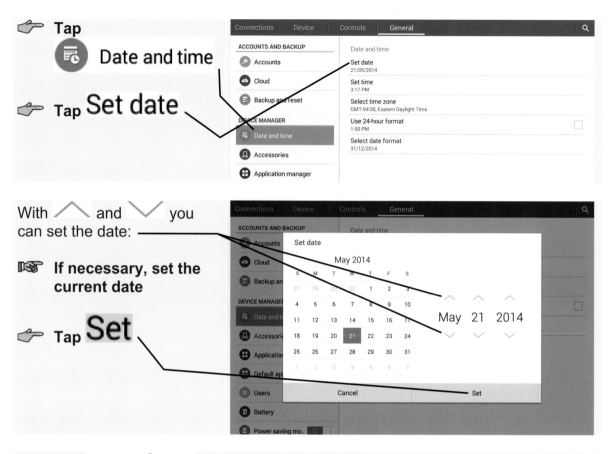

With ⌃ and ⌄ you can set the date:

☞ **If necessary, set the current date**

☞ **Tap** Set

☞ **Tap** Set time

☞ **If necessary, set the time**

☞ **Tap** Set

The default setting for the screen of the Samsung Galaxy Tab is that it rotates as you turn the device. Just try it:

☞ **Hold the Samsung Galaxy Tab in an upright position**

Now you will see that the image is displayed in portrait mode. You can lock the screen, so it will not rotate when you move the tablet. You do that like this:

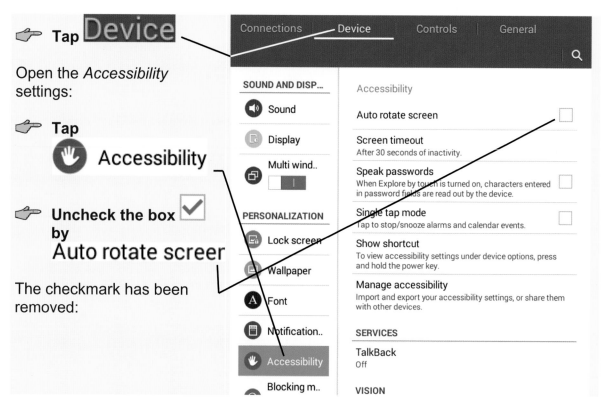

☞ **Tap** Device

Open the *Accessibility* settings:

☞ **Tap** ✋ Accessibility

☞ **Uncheck the box** ☑ **by** Auto rotate screer

The checkmark has been removed:

You can check to see if the new setting works:

☞ **Hold the Samsung Galaxy Tab in a horizontal (landscape) position**

Now you will see that the image on the Tab does not rotate. The screen has been locked in portrait mode. If you do want to rotate the screen of the Samsung Galaxy Tab when you turn the device, you can do this:

☞ **Hold the Samsung Galaxy Tab in an upright position**

☞ **Check the box** ☑ **by** Auto rotate screen

Now the screen will rotate as you turn the Samsung Galaxy Tab to a different position.

☞ **Hold the Samsung Galaxy Tab in a horizontal (landscape) position**

The image on the Samsung Galaxy Tab is displayed in landscape mode.

The *Accessibility* section contains more options than can be displayed on the screen.

☞ **Drag your finger upwards a bit, along the right-hand side of the screen** —————

This touch gesture will drag the list upwards, so you can see the bottom of the list. This gesture is called *scrolling*.

You can also do this the other way round:

☞ **Drag your finger downwards, along the right-hand side of the screen** —————

You will see the top of the list again.

Now you can leave the *Settings* app and go back to the home screen. For this you can use the Home button at the bottom of your tablet:

☞ **Press the Home button** ⬭

➥ **Please note:**
The screen shots for this book were made holding the Samsung Galaxy Tab in a horizontal (landscape) position. We recommend you also hold the Samsung Galaxy Tab in a horizontal position as you perform the operations described in this book. Otherwise, the screens on your Samsung Galaxy Tab will look slightly different from the images in this book.

1.5 Working with the Onscreen Keyboard

Your Samsung Galaxy Tab is equipped with a useful onscreen keyboard that is displayed whenever you need to type something. For example, when you take notes in the *Memo* app. Here is how you open this app:

You will see the apps installed on your tablet. This is how you open the *Memo* app:

Please note:

If you are using the Samsung Galaxy NotePro you will not see the *Memo* app, but instead you will see the *S Note* app. This app works in a different way. On the website accompanying this book, **www.visualsteps.com/samsungtab4**, you will find an additional PDF file about the *S Note* app under the *News* heading.

Please note:

While you are working with your Tab, you may see screens that provide additional information regarding the use of an app. You can read this information and tap

OK

afterwards.

Open a new, blank memo
page

☞ **Tap**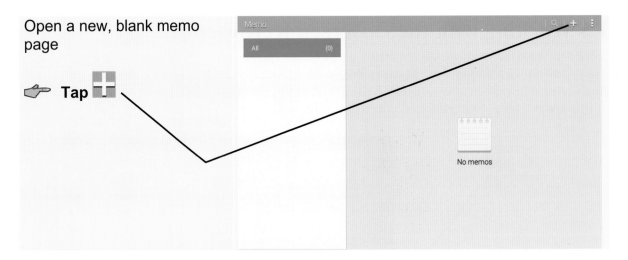

The onscreen keyboard works just like a regular keyboard. Only, you need to tap the keys instead of pressing them. Just try it:

⌨ **Type:**
   This is a test.

The ⏎ key has the same function as the Enter key on a regular keyboard. This is how you move down to the next line:

☞ **Tap** ⏎

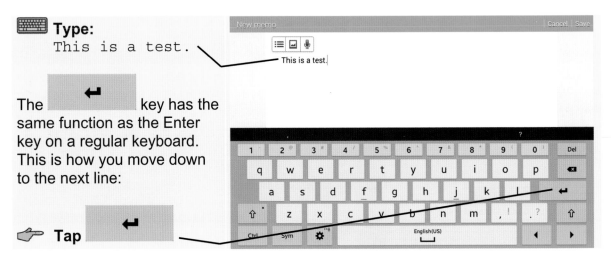

💡 Tip

Comma, period, exclamation mark, question mark
The comma and the exclamation mark share a key on the Tab's onscreen keyboard, just like the period and the question mark. This is how you type the lowest symbol on a key, for instance, a period:

👉 **Tap**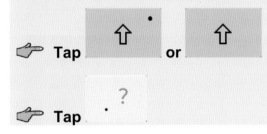

And this is how you type the uppermost symbol on a key, the question mark, for instance:

👉 **Tap** or

👉 **Tap**

💡 Tip

Capital letters
New sentences will automatically start with a capital letter. You can tell this by the

blue colored arrow and the capitals that appear on the onscreen keyboard when you move down a line.

This is how you type a capital in the middle of a sentence:

👉 **Tap** or

👉 **Tap the letter**

If you want to type the whole word in capital letters:

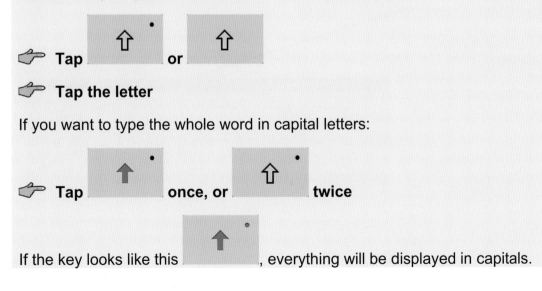

👉 **Tap** once, or twice

If the key looks like this , everything will be displayed in capitals.

Type the beginning of a simple sum:

Type: 12

In the default keyboard view, you will not see any special symbols. If you want to type the minus sign, you can use a different view:

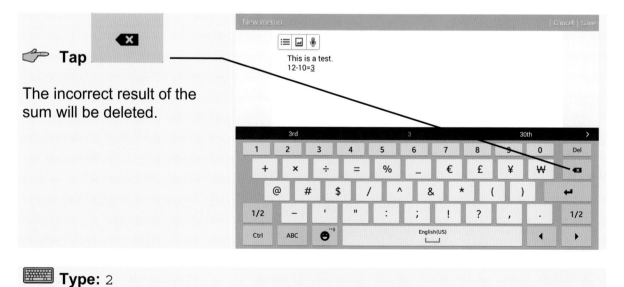

☞ **Tap** Sym

The keyboard view changes and you will now see the special symbols as well:

Type the remainder of the sum:

Type: -10=3

If you have typed the wrong character, you can correct this with the Backspace key:

☞ **Tap** ⌫

The incorrect result of the sum will be deleted.

Type: 2

Now the result is correct.

💡 Tip

Back to the default keyboard view

This is how you switch from the special symbols keyboard view to the default keyboard with the letters:

👉 **Tap** ABC

This is how you save the memo:

👉 **Tap** Save

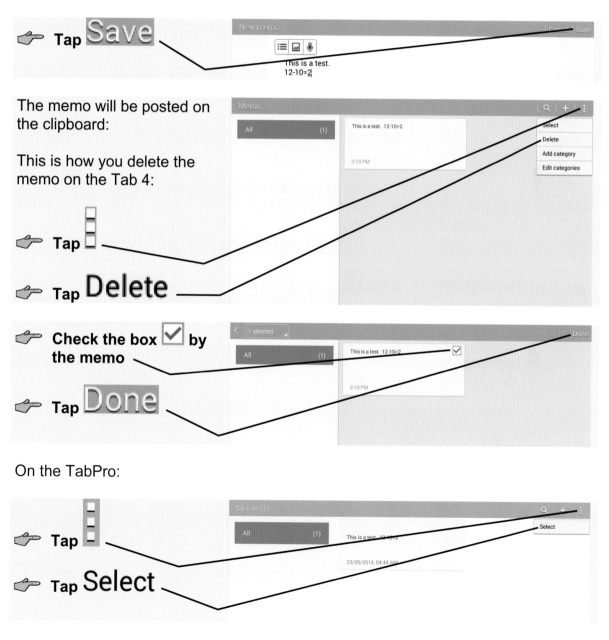

The memo will be posted on the clipboard:

This is how you delete the memo on the Tab 4:

👉 **Tap** ⋮

👉 **Tap** Delete

👉 **Check the box** ☑ **by the memo**

👉 **Tap** Done

On the TabPro:

👉 **Tap** ⋮

👉 **Tap** Select

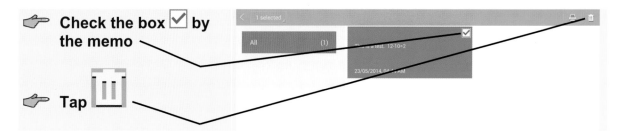

☞ **Check the box** ☑ **by the memo**

☞ **Tap** 🗑

The memo has been deleted:

At the bottom of the screen you can see how many memos you have deleted, and you can also undo these actions, if you wish:

1 deleted.	↺ Undo

This is how you quit working with the *Memo* app and go back to the home screen:

☞ **Press the Home button** ⬭

At this point you have practiced using some basic operations and touch gestures. There are other touch gestures, such as scrolling sideways, and zooming in and out. These will be discussed in the chapters where you need to use them.

1.6 Automatically Updating the Samsung Galaxy Tab

Samsung releases regular updates of the Samsung Galaxy Tab software. In these updates, problems are solved, or new functions are added. You can check whether the system automatically searches for software updates. In order to do this, you need to open the *Settings* app again. You can also do this directly from the home screen:

☞ **Tap** ▦ **and** Settings

The *Settings* app may already be placed on the home screen of your Tab.

☞ Tap General

☞ **Drag upwards along the left-hand side of the screen**

☞ Tap

ⓘ About device

☞ Tap
Software update

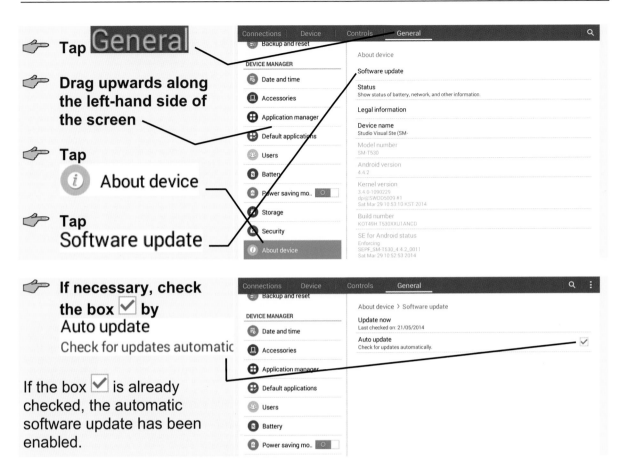

☞ **If necessary, check the box** ☑ **by Auto update**

Check for updates automatic

If the box ☑ is already checked, the automatic software update has been enabled.

The software update is activated. If a new version of the software is found, it will automatically be installed. Sometimes you will receive a message regarding this action. In that case:

☞ **If necessary, follow the instructions in the screens**

☞ **Press the Home button** ⬭

💡 **Tip**

Update through Samsung Kies 3
You can also install an update through *Samsung Kies 3*. In order to do this, first you will need to connect the Samsung Galaxy Tab to the computer. In the *Tips* at the end of this chapter you can read more about this subject.

1.7 Connect to the Internet through Wi-Fi

If you have access to a wireless network, you can connect to the Internet in the following way.

☛ Please note:

If you want to work through this section you will need to have access to a wireless network (Wi-Fi). If you do not have access, you can just read through this section.

Open the *Notification Panel*:

☞ **Drag your finger downwards, starting at the top of the screen**

The *Notification Panel* is displayed. You can connect to a Wi-Fi network like this:

☞ **Place your finger on**

Wi-Fi **, and hold it down for a moment** ——

A window with the available Wi-Fi networks will be opened:

☞ **Tap the network you want to use**

Please note: if a Wi-Fi network has already been set up, you will not see this window and the connection will be established right away. On the next page you can read more about this subject.

VisualSteps

If the network name is indicated as a secure network, such as Secured , you will need to enter a password in order to use it.

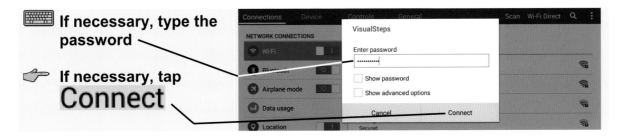

If necessary, type the password

If necessary, tap

Connect

A connection is established with the wireless network:

The symbol on the status bar indicates that there is a connection with a wireless network:

HELP! I do not see the status bar.

You may not see the status bar. This is how you display the status bar:

Drag your finger downwards, starting at the top of the screen

In future, a connection with known wireless networks will automatically be established when you turn on Wi-Fi. You can verify this, by turning the Wi-Fi off:

If necessary, display the status bar $\mathscr{D}$**38**

Open the *Notification Panel* $\mathscr{D}$**1**

Tap   Wi-Fi

Now Wi-Fi is turned off, and the button looks like this   Wi-Fi . You can re-connect again:

☞ **Tap**   Wi-Fi

The connection with the wireless network you have previously used is automatically established. And Wi-Fi is turned on again.

♀ **Tip**

Leave Wi-Fi turned on
It is a good idea to leave the Wi-Fi function turned on. This way, you will be permanently connected to the Internet, and you will receive all relevant updates, email messages, etcetera.

☞ **Press the Home button** ⬭

1.8 Connect to the Internet through a Mobile Data Network

If your Samsung Galaxy Tab is also suited for a 3G or 4G mobile data network as well as Wi-Fi, you can also connect to the Internet through this network. A mobile data network is useful when there is no Wi-Fi available. In order to use this network you need to have a SIM card with a data subscription, or a prepaid mobile Internet card. If you do not have a SIM card, you can just read through this section or skip to the following section.

💡 Tip

Mobile Internet

Since the Samsung Galaxy Tab does not have a simlock, you are free to choose your own mobile Internet service provider. Service providers such as AT&T, Time Warner Cable, and Verizon offer data subscriptions with a SIM card, and most cards are suitable for the Samsung Galaxy Tab, although you always need to check this. Prepaid mobile Internet cards are offered by T-mobile, AT&T, and Ready SIM, among other companies.

The fees and conditions are subject to regular changes. Visit the providers' websites for more information.

Before you can insert the SIM card, you need to turn off the Tab completely:

☞ **Press the Power/Lock button ⏻⟨   ⟩ until you see this screen**

☞ **Tap ⏻ Power off**

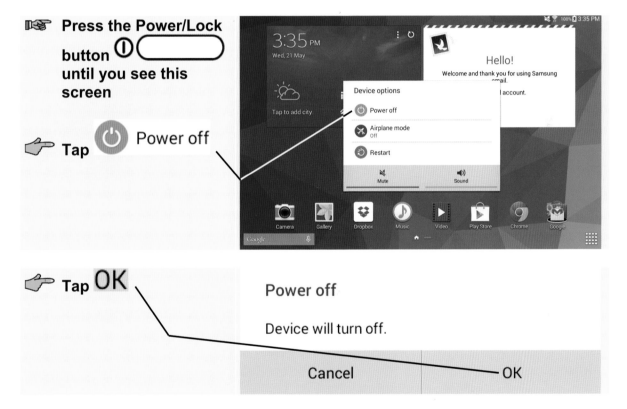

☞ **Tap OK**

Power off

Device will turn off.

Cancel   OK

☞ **Open the cover of the SIM card slot**

☞ **Insert the SIM card into the SIM card slot, make sure the gold-colored module is face down**

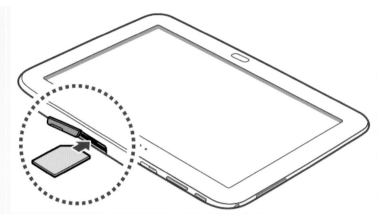

☞ **Press until the SIM card clicks into position**

Be careful not to touch the gold-colored part. This may damage the card.

Source: User manual Samsung Galaxy Tab 4

➦Please note:

This is what you do if you want to remove the card. First, press the SIM card downwards a little, then the SIM card will be released and move upwards. You will then be able to get hold of the card.

☞ **Close the cover of the SIM card slot**

Now you can turn on the Tab again:

☞ **Turn on the Samsung Galaxy Tab again** 👣4

The system will automatically connect to the mobile data network.

When the connection has been established, you will see the signal strength in the status bar, and the type of mobile data network **4G** ⬇ that is used:

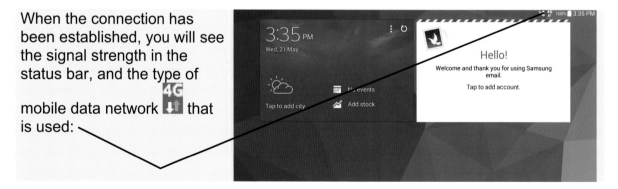

➦Please note:

If the connection is not established automatically, you may need to adjust a few more settings. Follow the instructions in the windows. You can also try to find additional information on your service provider's website.

You can temporarily turn off the Internet connection through the mobile data network, if necessary. For example, you can do this if you want to prevent your children (or grandchildren) from using your prepaid credit when they want to play games on your Samsung Galaxy Tab. You can turn off the connection like this:

☞ **Open the *Notification Panel* ✂¹**

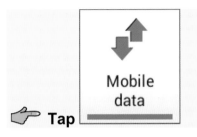

☞ **Tap**

You may see a warning about not being able to use certain apps through mobile networks:

☞ **Tap**

Now the use of mobile data has been turned off:

The status bar just displays

this symbol 📶⬇⬆:

This means that you are only connected to a Wi-Fi network.

🖐 **Please note:**

When you are using mobile data, the **Roaming** function is disabled by default. *Data roaming* means you are using the data network of a different provider, in case your own provider is unavailable. Be careful if you enable this function while abroad. You could incur huge data roaming fees.

Now you can activate the mobile data network again.

☞ **Open the *Notification Panel* ✂¹**

☞ **Tap**

☞ **Press the Home button**

1.9 Downloading and Installing Samsung Kies 3

You can also connect the device to your computer, laptop or notebook. With the use of the free *Samsung Kies 3* program you will be able to synchronize data, music, and other materials with your tablet. Synchronizing means making the content of your Tab identical to the content of the data in *Samsung Kies 3*.

First, you need to install *Samsung Kies 3* to your computer:

☞ **Open the www.samsung.com/us/kies website** 🔎⁶

Please note:

If you already have installed *Samsung Kies 3* to your computer, you can continue reading with *section 1.10 Connecting the Samsung Galaxy Tab to the Computer* on page 46.

Please note:

If you do not have a computer, you can just read through this section and continue with *section 1.12 Creating and Adding a Google Account* on page 50.

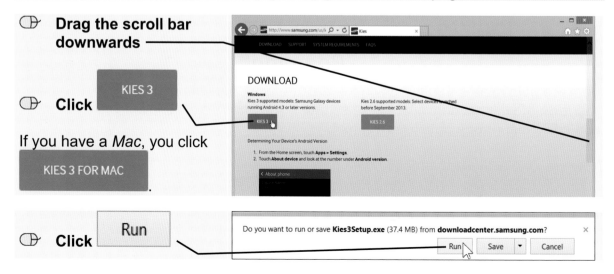

Ⓓ **Drag the scroll bar downwards**

Ⓓ **Click** KIES 3

If you have a *Mac*, you click

KIES 3 FOR MAC .

Ⓓ **Click** Run

You can see how much time remains for the download to be completed:

> 59% of Kies3Setup.exe downloaded   22 sec remaining
>
> Pause   Cancel   View downloads   ×

Your screen may turn dark and you will need to give permission to continue:

☞ **If necessary, give permission to continue**

✖ **HELP! I see a window regarding the installation of a codec.**

If this happens, you can read about the installation steps you need to take on page 235 in *Chapter 8 Music*.

In order to continue, you will need to accept the license agreement:

◦ **Check the box ✔ by
  I accept the terms o**

◦ **Click**

    Next >

> **Samsung Kies 3 - InstallShield Wizard**
>
> License agreement and choose destination location
>
> Please read the License Agreement.
> To continue installation, you must agree to the License Agreement.
>
> **Kies**
>
> Destination Folder
>
> C:\Program Files (x86)\Samsung\Kies3\   Change...
>
> License agreement
>
> Samsung Kies End User License Agreement
>
> Read carefully the Samsung Kies End User License Agreement (the "Agreement") before using Samsung Kies software as it contains important information.
>
> Samsung Kies is a software program to entertain various contents including music and video through digital devices manufactured by Samsung Electronics Co., Ltd. ("Samsung") including cell phones, MP3 players. You can easily transmit contents to digital devices through this Software.
>
> By using this Samsung Kies software, you agree to comply with the Agreement. Otherwise, you cannot use this software. When you click the "I accept the terms of the license agreement" to install the software, you are deemed to have consented to the
>
> ✔ I accept the terms of the license agreement
>
>   Next >   Cancel

You will see the progress of the installation process:

> C:\Program Files (x86)\Samsung\Kies3\FirmwareUpdate\mfcm90.dll
>
>   Cancel

The installation continues. This may take a little while. You do not need to open the program right away:

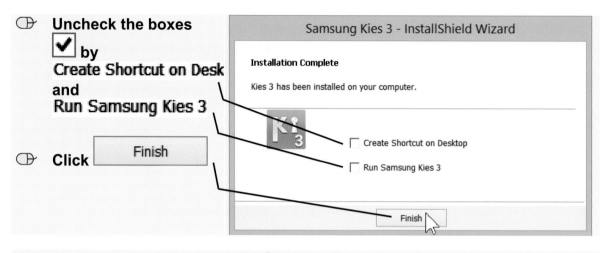

☞ **Close your Internet browser** 🐾**8**

1.10 Connecting the Samsung Galaxy Tab to the Computer

Before you connect the Galaxy Tab to the computer, open the program *Samsung Kies 3* on your computer first. In *Windows 8.1*, you can do that from the Start screen:

⌨ **Type:** `Kies`

You may see this window:

☞ **If necessary, click**

| Update |

The update will be installed.

You see the progress of the update operation:

| **Kies Update** |

| Kies_3.2.14034_17.exe (699.8 KB/Second)   13% |

Version : 3.2.14034.17.0
Date updated : 2014-05-23

| Cancel |

During the installation process, you may need to give permission to continue:

☞ **If necessary, give permission to continue**

You may see a message telling you that you need to uninstall the previous version of *Samsung Kies 3* if you want to install the latest version:

☞ **Click** | Yes |

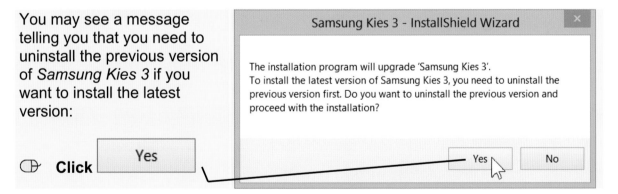

Samsung Kies 3 - InstallShield Wizard

The installation program will upgrade 'Samsung Kies 3'.
To install the latest version of Samsung Kies 3, you need to uninstall the previous version first. Do you want to uninstall the previous version and proceed with the installation?

| Yes | No |

You will see the progress of the installation operation.

Finally, you will see the *Samsung Kies 3* home screen:

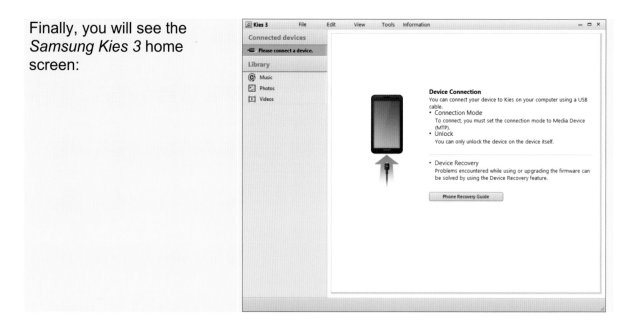

Now you can connect the Tab. You do that like this:

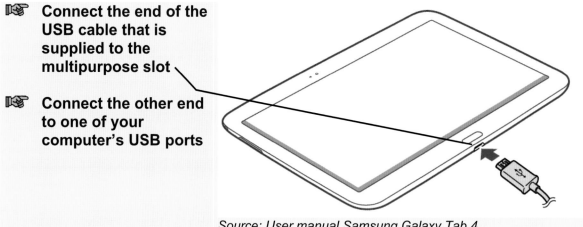

☞ **Connect the end of the USB cable that is supplied to the multipurpose slot**

☞ **Connect the other end to one of your computer's USB ports**

Source: User manual Samsung Galaxy Tab 4

You will probably see a window with a message about the installation of the device. A few seconds later the device will be ready to use.

You may also see the *AutoPlay* window:

☞ **If necessary, close the *AutoPlay* window** &⁸

Meanwhile, you will also see the connection with the Samsung Galaxy Tab appear in the *Samsung Kies 3* window:

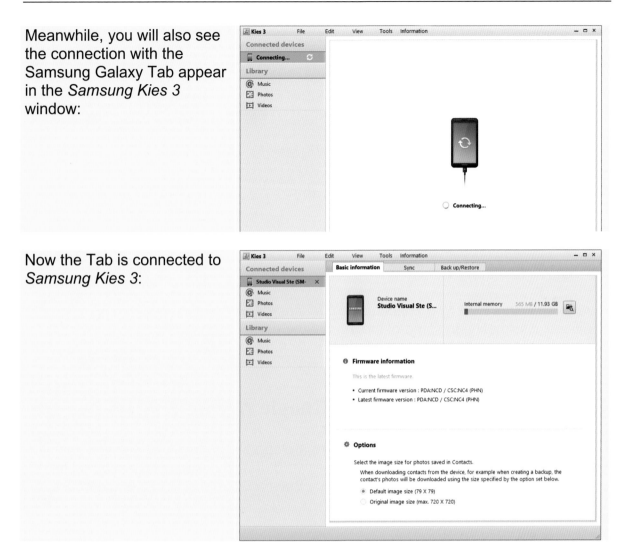

Now the Tab is connected to *Samsung Kies 3*:

1.11 Safely Disconnecting the Samsung Galaxy Tab

If you want to disconnect the Samsung Galaxy Tab, you need to make sure no data is being transferred between the device and the computer. If that is the case, the data on your computer may be damaged. This is how you break the connection between the Tab and *Samsung Kies 3*:

By the name of your Tab, click ✕

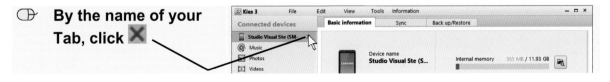

The Samsung Galaxy Tab has disappeared from the *Samsung Kies 3* window, and you will see the home screen again:

Now you can safely disconnect the Samsung Galaxy Tab:

☞ **Disconnect the Samsung Galaxy Tab** 🐾**13**

You can close *Samsung Kies 3*:

☞ **Close *Samsung Kies 3*** 🐾**7**

Further on in this book you will be using *Samsung Kies 3* again. You can also find additional information in some of the *Tips* at the end of this chapter, and in other chapters, regarding the things you can do with *Samsung Kies 3*.

1.12 Creating and Adding a Google Account

Many *Google* and *Android* functions require a *Google* account. A *Google* account is a combination of an email address and a password. In this section you are going to create a new *Google* account. If you already have a *Google* account, you can use it with your Tab.

☞ **Unlock the Samsung Galaxy Tab** 🐾**9**

☞ **Tap** ⊞ **and** ⚙ Settings

☞ **If necessary, tap** General

☞ **Tap ➕ Add account**

Select the *Google* account:

☞ **Tap**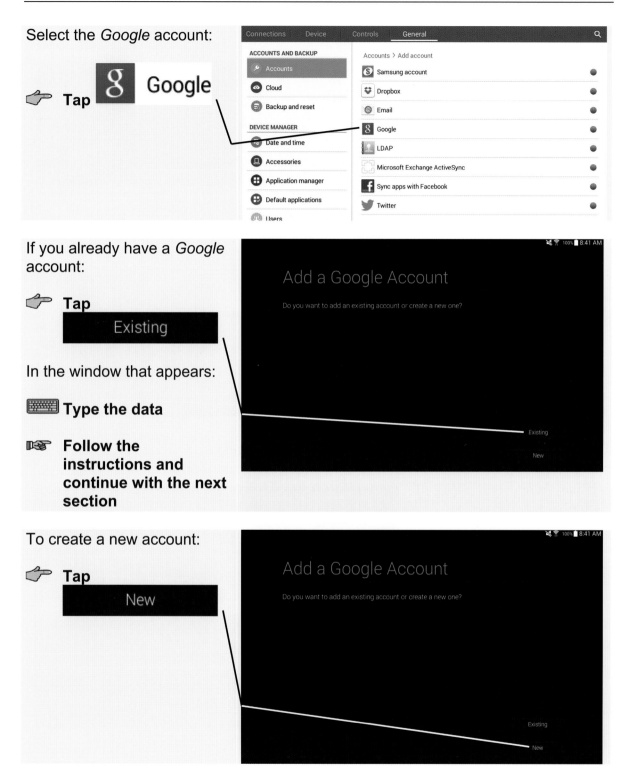

If you already have a *Google* account:

☞ **Tap**

> Existing

In the window that appears:

⌨ **Type the data**

☞ **Follow the instructions and continue with the next section**

To create a new account:

☞ **Tap**

> New

First, enter your first and last name:

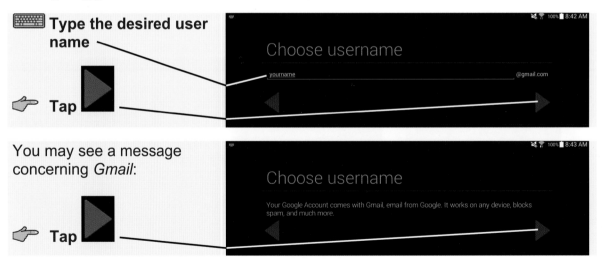

👉 **Tap** First

⌨ **Type your first name**

👉 **Tap** Next

⌨ **Type your last name**

👉 **Tap** ▶

You can choose your own user name. This name consists of an email address ending in @gmail.com.

⌨ **Type the desired user name**

👉 **Tap** ▶

You may see a message concerning *Gmail*:

👉 **Tap** ▶

HELP! User name is already in use.

If the user name you have entered is already being used by someone else, you will see this message `The username isn't available.`.

Tap `Touch for suggestions`

Google will provide some suggestions for available user names:

Tap a name in the list

If you decide not to use the suggestion, you can type a different name.

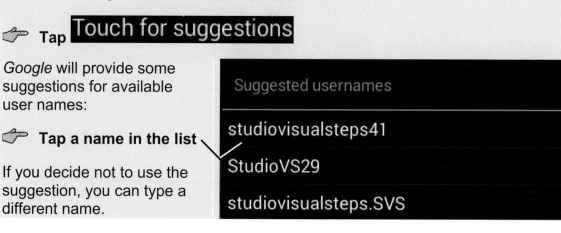

The password that goes with your *Google* account needs to consist of at least eight characters. It is recommended to use a combination of capital and lowercase letters, numbers, and even special characters for your password.

Type the desired password

Tap

Done (Tab 4) or

Next (TabPro)

If necessary, tap `Re-type password`

Re-type the password

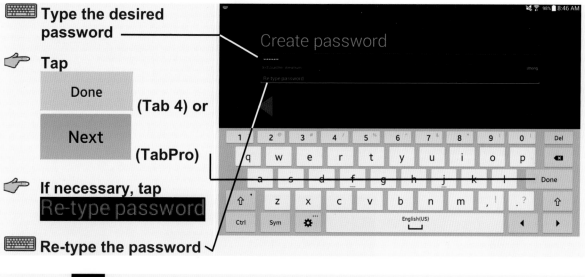

Tap

You can choose to set some recovery options, in case you forget your password. If this happens, you will receive a text or email message (at a different email address) regarding the restoration of your password. You can set up a recovery option:

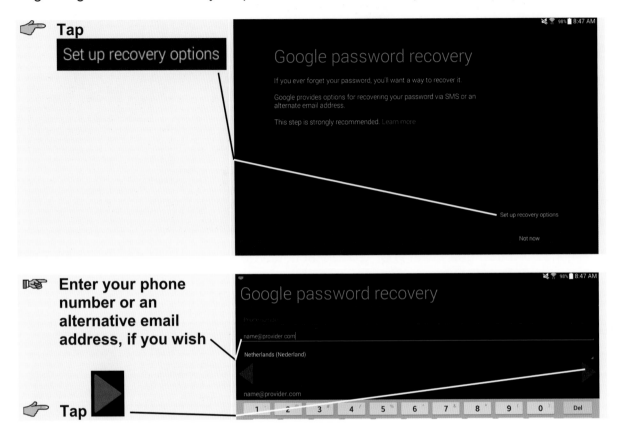

Tap
Set up recovery options

Enter your phone number or an alternative email address, if you wish

Tap

You may see a screen regarding the creation of a backup copy. It is a good idea to leave this option enabled. This way, you will create a safety backup copy of your tablet through your *Google* account, in case something goes wrong.

At the bottom of the screen:

Tap

In order to continue, you need to agree to the *Google* service conditions and the privacy policy:

You will see a box with characters you need to copy:

You will be asked whether you want to upgrade to *Google+*. This is *Google's* social network site. For now this will not be necessary:

A connection will be established with *Google* and your account will be saved.

You may see a screen regarding games or other amusement. For now you can skip this screen:

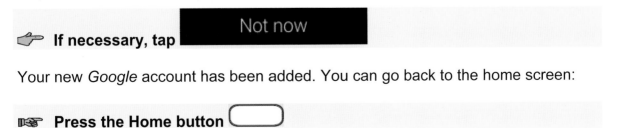

Your new *Google* account has been added. You can go back to the home screen:

☞ **Press the Home button** ⬭

1.13 Locking or Turning Off the Samsung Galaxy Tab

Once you have finished working on the Samsung Galaxy Tab, you can either lock or completely turn off the tablet. If you lock it, the Samsung Galaxy Tab will still be turned on, but will consume less energy. If you have turned off Wi-Fi or the mobile data network, the Tab will hardly use any power at all. This is how you lock the Samsung Galaxy Tab:

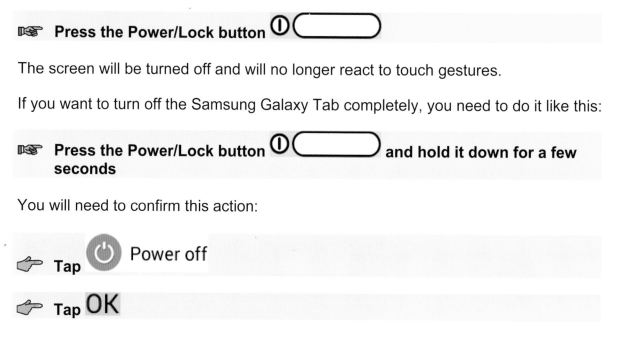

Press the Power/Lock button

The screen will be turned off and will no longer react to touch gestures.

If you want to turn off the Samsung Galaxy Tab completely, you need to do it like this:

Press the Power/Lock button **and hold it down for a few seconds**

You will need to confirm this action:

Tap **Power off**

Tap OK

The Samsung Galaxy Tab will turn off.

In future, you can choose whether to lock or turn off the Samsung Galaxy Tab. In this chapter you have become acquainted with the main components of the Samsung Galaxy Tab and learned some of the basic operations for using this device. You can find additional information in the *Background Information* and *Tips* sections.

1.14 Background Information

Dictionary

Airplane mode	If your Tab is set to this mode, you will not have access to the Internet and will not be able to use any Bluetooth devices.
Android	A mobile operating system for cell phones, smartphones, tablets and other devices. *Android* is not linked to a single, specific manufacturer. *Google* places *Android* at the disposal of mobile device manufacturers for free. Many manufacturers of smartphones and tablets install their own user interfaces to their devices. This means that tablets from different manufacturers will look and function differently, even though they use the same version of *Android*.
App	Short for *application*, a program for the Samsung Galaxy Tab.
App icons	Colored symbols that can be used to open various apps on the Samsung Galaxy Tab.
Back button	The ⮌ button on the Tab. It lets you go back to the previous screen.
Bluetooth	An open wireless technology standard for exchanging data between devices over short distances. For example, you can use Bluetooth to connect a wireless keyboard or a headset to the Samsung Galaxy Tab.
Dropbox	With this app you can easily store and share photos and documents. You can take a picture with your Tab, save it, and open it on your computer, provided you have installed *Dropbox* on your computer as well.
EDGE	Short for *Enhanced Data Rates for GSM Evolution*. This is an extension of GPRS, which enables higher speed rates for data transmission. The EDGE service is widely available in the USA, but in Europe there is limited availability in some countries.

- Continue on the next page -

Firmware	Software that is embedded in the hardware. The name firmware indicates that the content is quite firm and exists on the boundary between software (easily re-writable and accessible) and hardware (basically unchangeable).
Google account	A combination of a user name and a password, that provides access to *Google* and *Android* functions and services.
GPRS	Short for *General Packet Radio Service*. A technology that offers an extension of the existing gsm network. This technology enables users to send and receive mobile data much faster, more efficiently and cheaper.
Home button	The ⬭ button on the Tab (also called Home key) with which you can go back to the home screen. You can also use this button to wake up the Tab from sleep mode.
Home screen	The screen filled with widgets and app icons, that you see when you turn on and unlock the Samsung Galaxy Tab.
Library	The component on *Samsung Kies 3* where you can store and manage your music, photos, videos and contacts.
Location services	With location services, apps such as *Maps* can collect and use data regarding your current location. The collected location data is not linked to your personal data.
Lock	You can lock the Samsung Galaxy Tab by turning off the screen with the Power/Lock button, when you do not need to use the device. If the Samsung Galaxy Tab is locked, nothing will happen when you touch the screen. Music playback will continue as usual. And you will still be able to use the volume control buttons.
Lock screen	The screen that appears when you turn on the Samsung Galaxy Tab. You will need to unlock the Tab on this screen, before you can use the device.
Micro SD card	A Micro SD memory card, sized 15 x 11 x 1 mm (about the size of a fingernail), often used in smartphones and tablets. The Tab is equipped with a Micro SD card slot. By inserting a Micro SD card you can expand the Tab's memory.

- Continue on the next page -

Play Store	An online store where you can download free and paid apps.
Power/Lock button	The ⏻◯⬭⬭⬭ button, with which you can lock, unlock, and turn on or turn off the Samsung Galaxy Tab.
Recent apps button	The ▭ button on the Tab that lets you quickly switch between recently used apps.
Roaming, data roaming	Using the mobile data network of a different service provider, in case your own provider's network is not available. This may result in high expenses if you do this abroad.
Samsung account	A combination of a user name and a password with which users can gain access to specific services offered by Samsung.
Samsung Galaxy Tab	The Samsung Galaxy Tab is a portable multimedia device (tablet computer) made by Samsung. The tablet has a 10.1 inch, 8 inch or 7 inch multi-touch screen. The Samsung Galaxy NotePro also has a 12.2 inch screen.
Samsung Kies 3	A program with which you can manage the content of the Samsung Galaxy Tab and other Samsung devices.
SIM card	SIM stands for *Subscriber Identity Module*. The SIM card is the (small) chip card that is provided by your mobile service provider and that you need to insert in your tablet or cell phone. Usually you will need to do this yourself.
Simlock	A simlock is a lock that has been installed in a cell phone, or any other mobile device, and is intended to prevent the user from inserting a SIM card issued by a different phone service provider. These simlocks are often installed because the phones are offered at very low prices (supported and paid for by the providers) in order to attract and retain customers. The Samsung Galaxy Tab Wi-Fi + 3G/4G is simlock free.
Smart stay	If the *Smart stay* option is enabled, the screen will remain turned on as long as you are watching it.

- Continue on the next page -

Synchronize	Literally, this means equalizing. When you synchronize your Tab with the content of your *Samsung Kies 3 Library*, the content of the Tab is equalized to the content of your *Library*. If you delete files or apps from your *Library*, these will also be deleted from the Samsung Galaxy Tab, the next time you synchronize the devices again.
Tablet computer, tablet	A tablet computer is a computer with no separate casing or keyboard. It can be fully operated through the multi-touch screen.
Timeout screen	A function that will turn off and lock the Samsung Galaxy Tab by default after 30 seconds of inactivity.
Widget	Small applications that provide information and useful functions.
Wi-Fi	Wireless network for the Internet.
3G	The third generation of data transmission standards for cell phones and tablets. Because of the higher speed, 3G offers more options than previous standards. With 3G you can make use of services such as making phone calls through the Internet.
4G	4G is the fourth generation of mobile data transmission standards for cell phones and tablets. With 4G you can make use of services such as making phone calls through the Internet, among other things. It is faster than 3G.

Source: User manual Samsung Galaxy Tab, Wikipedia

1.15 Tips

Tip

Set up sounds

Your Tab makes several noises when certain events occur. For instance, when you receive an email or a notification, or when you are using the keyboard. You can determine which sounds you do and do not want to hear. You can do this with the *Settings* app:

☞ **Open the *Settings* app** 🐾5

☞ **If necessary, tap** Device

☞ **Tap** 🔊 **Sound**

Here you can set the sound signal for notifications, among other things:

If you scroll upwards, you can enable or disable system sounds, such as keyboard sounds.

Tip

Timeout screen

By default, your Samsung Galaxy Tab will be locked after 30 seconds of inactivity. This setting will save battery energy, but you might find it easier to keep the Samsung Galaxy Tab unlocked for a little while longer:

☞ **Open the *Settings* app** 🐾5

☞ **If necessary, tap** Device

☞ **Tap** 🔲 **Display**

☞ **Tap** Screen timeout

- Continue on the next page -

You will see a window where you can set a different time period:

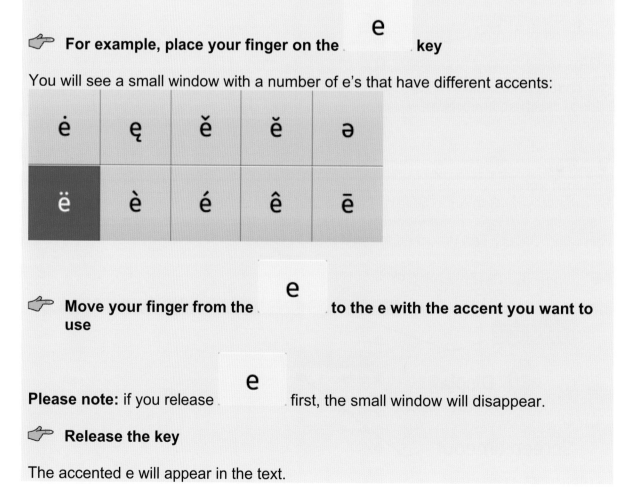

☞ **Tap the desired setting**

💡 Tip

Accented letters

The letters that contain accents are not displayed on the keyboard. Yet you can still type them:

☞ **For example, place your finger on the** e **key**

You will see a small window with a number of e's that have different accents:

ė	ę	ĕ	ĕ	ə
ë	è	é	ê	ē

☞ **Move your finger from the** e **to the e with the accent you want to use**

Please note: if you release e first, the small window will disappear.

☞ **Release the key**

The accented e will appear in the text.

💡 Tip

Typing with Google voice control

The Tab is equipped with the *Google Voice* function. This function converts speech to text:

☞ **Open a new memo** 𝒬𝒪11

☞ **Display the status bar** 𝒬𝒪38

☞ **Open the *Notification Panel*** 𝒬𝒪1

👉 **Tap** Select input method / Samsung keyboard , Google voice typing

☞ **Speak clearly and not too fast**

The text appears:

Here you see the default language is used for entering text:

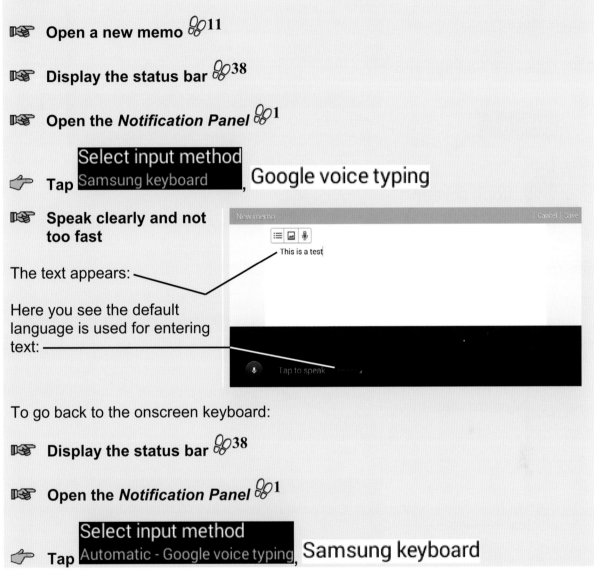

To go back to the onscreen keyboard:

☞ **Display the status bar** 𝒬𝒪38

☞ **Open the *Notification Panel*** 𝒬𝒪1

👉 **Tap** Select input method / Automatic - Google voice typing, Samsung keyboard

♀ Tip

Lock the screen with a pattern

When you turn on the tablet, you drag your finger over the screen, in order to unlock the device. Of course, anyone can do this. But you can protect your tablet even better. For example, with a PIN code, a password, or a pattern. You can set a pattern like this:

☞ Open the *Settings* app 🐾5

☞ If necessary, tap *Device*

☞ Tap *Lock screen*

☞ Tap *Screen lock Swipe*

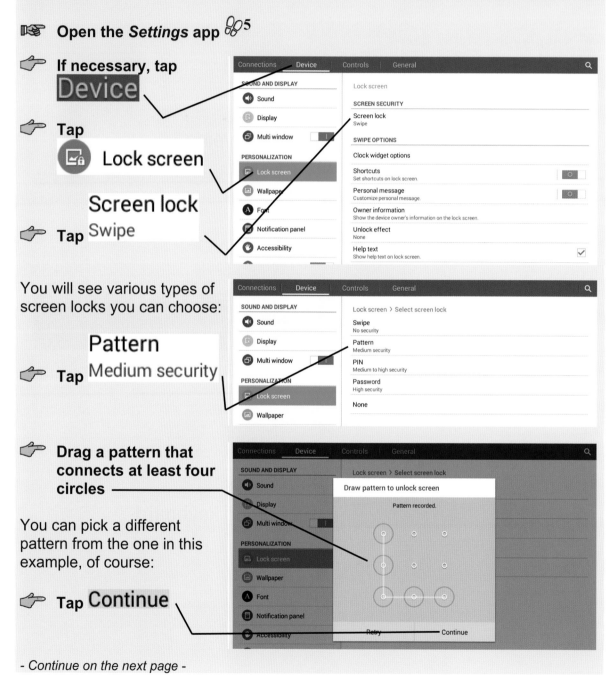

You will see various types of screen locks you can choose:

☞ Tap *Pattern Medium security*

☞ **Drag a pattern that connects at least four circles**

You can pick a different pattern from the one in this example, of course:

☞ Tap **Continue**

- Continue on the next page -

☞ **Drag the same pattern once again** ——

☞ **Tap Confirm** —

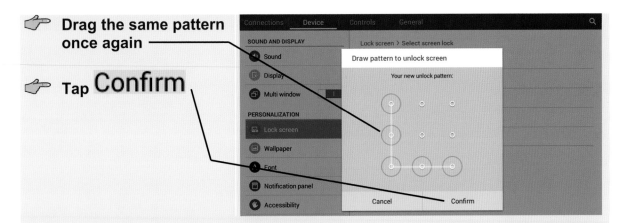

By way of an extra security check, you will be asked to choose a PIN code consisting of four digits. With this PIN code you can unlock your tablet as well, in case you have forgotten the pattern:

⌨ **Type a PIN code** ——

☞ **Tap Done**

⌨ **Re-type the PIN code** ——

☞ **Tap Done**

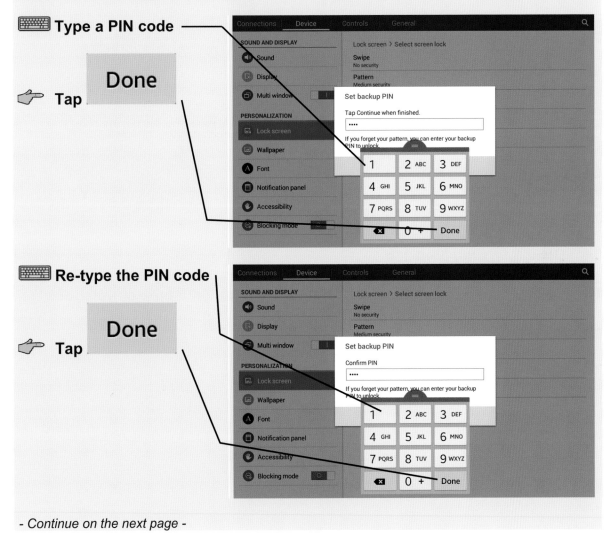

- Continue on the next page -

You have just changed your
tablet's security settings:

Connections	Device	Controls	General	🔍

SOUND AND DISPLAY

🔊 Sound

🖥 Display

📱 Multi window   [▮▯]

PERSONALIZATION

📋 Lock screen

🖼 Wallpaper

🅰 Font

Lock screen

SCREEN SECURITY

Screen lock
Secured with pattern

SECURED WITH PATTERN

Clock widget options

Personal message   [○]
Customize personal message.

Owner information
Show the device owner's information on the lock screen.

Now you are going to check if it works:

☞ **Press the Home button** ⬭

☞ **Lock your Samsung Galaxy Tab** 👣^{14}

☞ **Unlock your Samsung Galaxy Tab** 👣^{9}

You will see the lock screen:

 Drag your pattern

💡 **Tip**

Create a backup with Samsung Kies 3
In the *Samsung Kies 3* program you can manually create a backup copy of your
Samsung Galaxy Tab. Here is how you do that:

☞ **Open *Samsung Kies 3*** 👣^{12}

☞ **Connect the Samsung Galaxy Tab to the computer, laptop or notebook**

☞ **If necessary, close the Help window** 👣^{18}

👉 **Click the** [Back up/Restore] **tab**

- Continue on the next page -

☞ **Check the box ✅ by the items you want to include in the backup**

Or:

☞ **Check the box ✅ by Select all items**

☞ **Click**

Backup

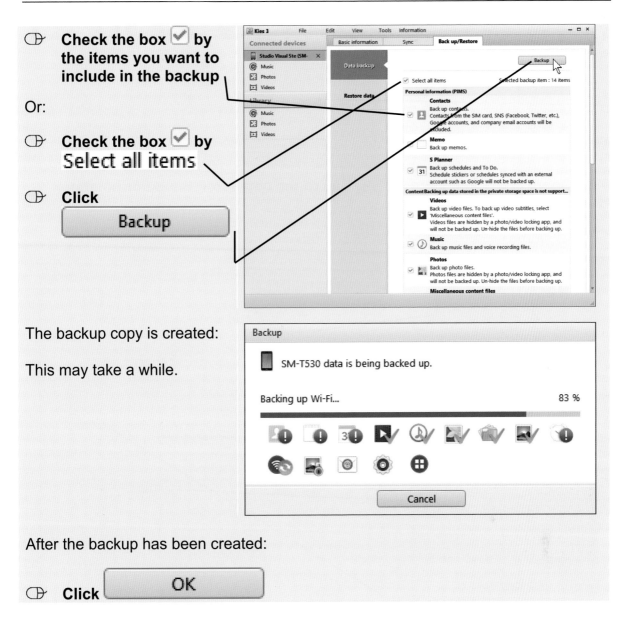

The backup copy is created:

This may take a while.

After the backup has been created:

☞ **Click** OK

💡 **Tip**

Restore a backup with Samsung Kies 3
If you experience any problems with your tablet, you can restore a previously created backup. Here is how you do that:

☞ **Open *Samsung Kies 3*** 🔗^{12}

☞ **Connect the Samsung Galaxy Tab to the computer, laptop or notebook**

👉 **Click the** ⬛ Back up/Restore **tab**

👉 **Click**
Restore data

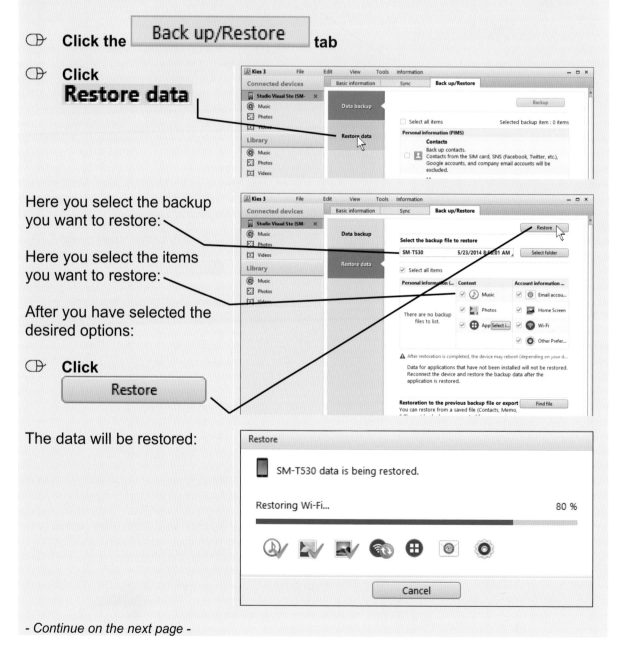

Here you select the backup you want to restore:

Here you select the items you want to restore:

After you have selected the desired options:

👉 **Click**
⬛ Restore

The data will be restored:

- Continue on the next page -

You may now see some windows regarding the import of contacts. If this is the case, check the box ☑ by the desired option(s) and click [OK].

After the backup has been restored:

☞ **Click** [OK]

Your Samsung Galaxy Tab will be re-started.

☞ **Disconnect the Samsung Galaxy Tab** 🐾¹³

☞ **Close *Samsung Kies 3* 🐾⁷**

💡 **Tip**
Upgrading the Tab firmware through Samsung Kies 3
Previously, you have read how to download and install a software update to your Tab using Wi-Fi. With *Samsung Kies 3* you can upgrade the *firmware* on your device. Firmware is software that is embedded in the hardware. The name 'firmware' indicates that the content is firm and is something between software (easy to overwrite) and hardware (basically not overwritable).

☞ **Open *Samsung Kies 3* 🐾¹²**

☞ **Connect the Samsung Galaxy Tab to the computer, laptop or notebook**

If you see this message
This is the latest firmwa
you do not need to do
anything:

If an update is available:

☞ **Create a backup of the data on your tablet as described in the previous *Tip***

☞ **Click** [Firmware-upgrade]

☞ **Follow the instructions in the windows**

💡 Tip

Smart stay

The Tab has a *Smart stay* function. This means that the Tab can detect whether you are watching the screen or not. If you are not watching the screen, the screen will turn dark after a while, and you will need to unlock the device.

You can easily enable and disable the *Smart stay* function. You can do this in the *Notification Panel*:

👉 **Open the *Notification Panel* ✂️¹**

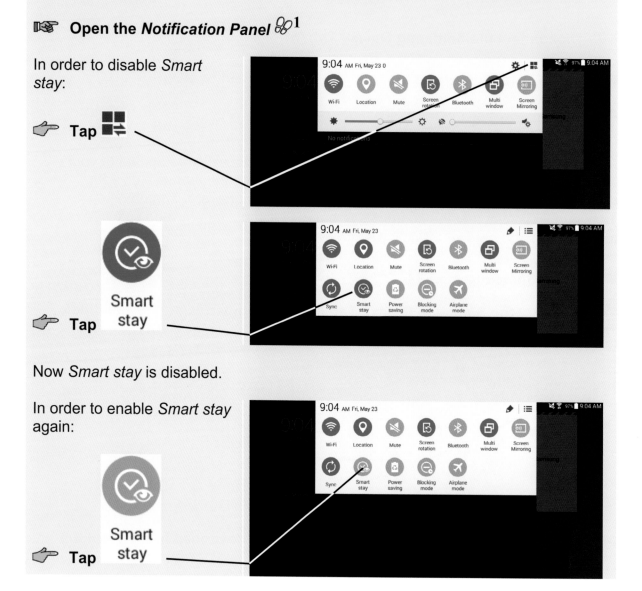

In order to disable *Smart stay*:

👉 **Tap** 🔳

👉 **Tap Smart stay**

Now *Smart stay* is disabled.

In order to enable *Smart stay* again:

👉 **Tap Smart stay**

2. Using Email on Your Tablet

Your Samsung Galaxy Tab is equipped with two standard apps for using email: *Gmail* and *Email*. The *Email* app allows you to use the email services from any provider you like. With both apps you can write, send and receive email messages, just like you do on your computer.

In this chapter you will learn how to use the *Email* app. To start using this app, you must first add an email account.

It is easy to use your Samsung Galaxy Tab to compose an email. In this chapter you will practice doing this. You will learn how to select, copy, cut, and paste text on the screen of the Samsung Galaxy Tab. You will also get acquainted with the *Predictive text* function.

Later we will explain how to send, receive and delete email messages.

In this chapter you will learn how to:

- set up an email account in the *Email* app;
- use the *Predictive text* function;
- cut, paste and copy text;
- send an email;
- receive an email;
- move an email to the *Trash*;
- permanently delete an email.

➥ Please note:

While you are using your Tab, you may see some screens that provide additional information about the operation of an app or the keyboard. You can read the information and tap **Done** or **OK** afterwards.

2.1 Opening Email and Adding an Email Account

In this section you are going to open the *Email* app, and you will learn how to add an Internet service provider's account, for instance, AT&T or T-Mobile. In order to do this, you will need to have the server data, the user name, and the password sent to you by your service provider. If you have an email address ending in hotmail.com, live.com, or gmail.com, you can use any of them to set up an email address for your Tab.

☞ Unlock or turn on the Samsung Galaxy Tab 🐾⁹

Open the *Email* app in the screen with the full list of apps. In the bottom right-hand corner of the screen:

☞ Tap ⊞

☞ Tap Email

You will see a screen where you need to enter some basic information concerning your email account. You can use the onscreen keyboard of your Tab to type this information:

Type your email address

Type your password

After you have entered the information:

☞ Tap 〉

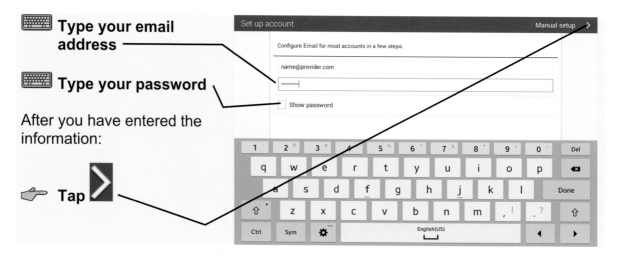

Now you may need to choose whether you want to set up your account as an *IMAP*, *POP*, or *Microsoft Exchange ActiveSync* account:

- IMAP stands for *Internet Message Access Protocol*. This means that you manage your messages on the mail server. Messages that have been read will still be stored on the mail server, until you delete them. IMAP is useful if you want to manage your email on multiple computers or devices. Your mailbox will look the same on all the devices you use.
  In case you have created folders to arrange your messages, these folders will be present on all the other computers too, and on your Tab. If you want to use IMAP, you need to set up your email account as an IMAP account on all your devices.
- POP stands for *Post Office Protocol*, which is the traditional way of managing email. When you collect your mail, the messages will immediately be deleted from the server. Although the default setting on your Tab for POP accounts is to save a copy of your emails on the server, even after you have retrieved your messages. This means you can always retrieve your messages on your computer as well.
- *Microsoft Exchange ActiveSync*. This technologies enables you to use your Tab to work with the same email, calendars, tasks, and contacts as in the *Microsoft Outlook* email program (part of the *Microsoft Office* suite). This way, you can also access your data when you are travelling. Moreover, *ActiveSync* makes sure that the information on the Tab and in *Microsoft Outlook* is the same. We will not discuss this technology any further in this book.

☞ **If necessary, tap POP3 account or IMAP account**

What type of account?

POP3 account

IMAP account

Microsoft Exchange ActiveSync

If you do not see the previous screen:

☞ **Tap** ⏩ **and continue on the next page**

Now you can enter the information you have received from your Internet service provider:

⌨ **By Username, type the user name**

⌨ **By Password, type your password**

Incoming server settings ‹ | ›

Username
username

Password
••••••••

IMAP server
imap.provider.com

Security type

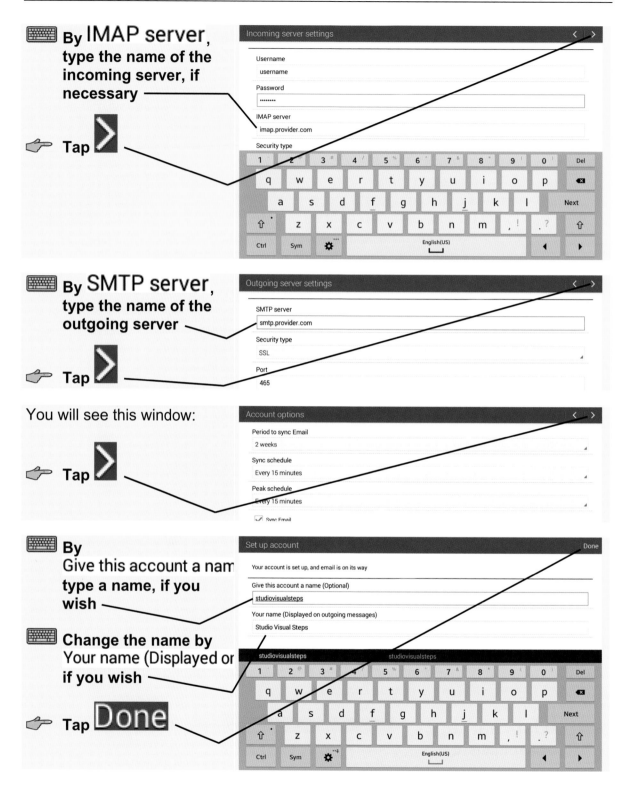

By IMAP server, type the name of the incoming server, if necessary ——

☞ Tap

By SMTP server, type the name of the outgoing server ——

☞ Tap

You will see this window:

☞ Tap

By
Give this account a nam type a name, if you wish ——

Change the name by Your name (Displayed or if you wish ——

☞ Tap Done

You will see the *Email* screen:

In this example, there already is an email in the inbox:

You may not see any messages on your own Tab.

2.2 Sending an Email

To practice using email you can write and send an email message to yourself. Open a new, blank email:

In the top right-hand corner of the screen:

☞ **Tap** ✏️

A new message is opened.

⌨️ **By To, type your email address**

💡 **Tip**

CC and BCC

With the CC and BCC options you can send a copy of an email message. If you use BCC, the recipients will not be visible to one another. If you use CC, all the recipients will be able to see the names of the other recipients. If you want to use this option, you tap **∨** and enter the email addresses of the recipient(s) on the relevant line.

☉ Tip

Contacts

If any contacts have been added to the *Contacts* app, you will see a list of names and corresponding email addresses, after you have typed the first two letters of a name. You can quickly add the email address by tapping the name you want to use. In *Chapter 4 Managing Contacts, Calendar and Widgets* you will learn how to fill the contacts' list in the *Contacts* app.

⌨ By **Subject**, **type:**

Test

While you are typing, the bar above the keyboard will display all kinds of suggestions for the word you are typing: ⎯⎯⎯

This function is called *Predictive text*. While you type, entire words are recommended on the basis of the letters you have already typed. This can save you a lot of typing time. Just try this with the first part of the word 'computer'.

☞ **Tap the white text box**

⌨ **Type:** Compu

You will see various suggestions. This is how you accept a suggestion:

☞ **Tap** Computer

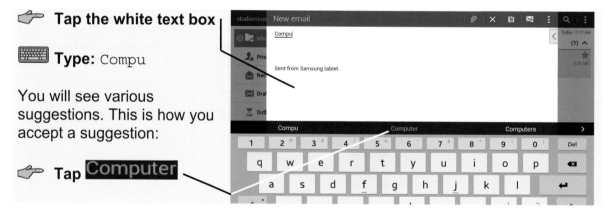

☉ Tip

Accept a correction

A suggested blue correction will also be accepted if you type a period, comma or another punctuation mark.

☉ Tip

Disable predictive text

In the *Tips* at the end of this chapter you can read how to disable the *Predictive text* function while you are typing.

If you are not satisfied with what you have typed, you can quickly delete the text with the Backspace key:

👉 **Press your finger to** ⌫ **until the text is deleted**

⌨️ **Type:** The screen of the Samsung Galaxy Tab is touch-sensitive.

👉 **Tap** ↵ **twice**

In the *Email* app you can also copy, cut and paste text. You can do this with a single word, multiple words or the entire text. This is how you select a word:

👉 **Press your finger to the word** Galaxy

Now the word is selected and you will see blue handles below the word:

👉 **Release the screen**

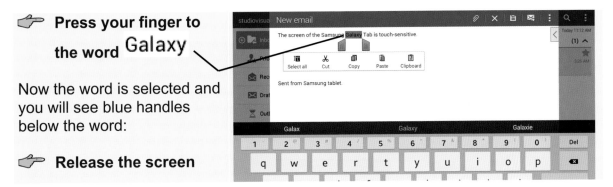

By using the handles you can adjust the selection. For example, you can select the text 'Samsung Galaxy Tab':

👉 **Drag the left handle** 📱 **across** Samsung

👉 **Drag the right handle** 📱 **across** Tab

The full name has been selected:

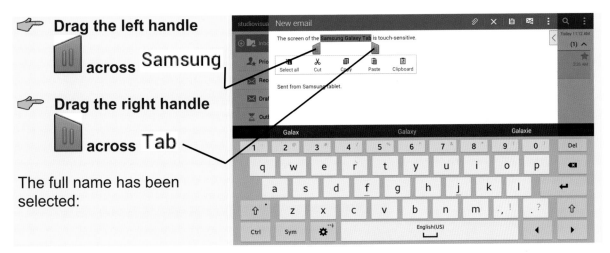

You can cut, copy or replace the selected words. To copy the words:

The words have been copied to the clipboard. This is how you paste them in the text:

👉 **Place your finger below the text**

You will see a blue arrow:

👉 **Release the screen**

👉 **Tap** Paste

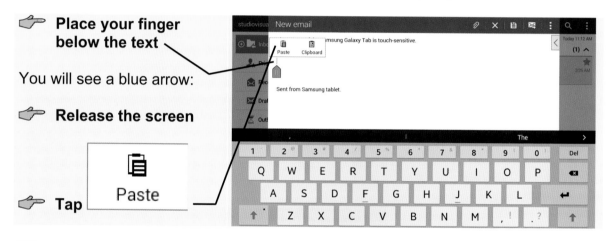

The copied text has been inserted below the first line:

Now you can send your test email:

👉 **Tap**

Your email message is sent, and if the sound on the Samsung Galaxy Tab is turned on, you will hear a sound signal.

2.3 Receiving an Email

You will receive your message very soon after you have sent it. It will appear at the top of your *Inbox*.

The number indicates that there are unread messages:

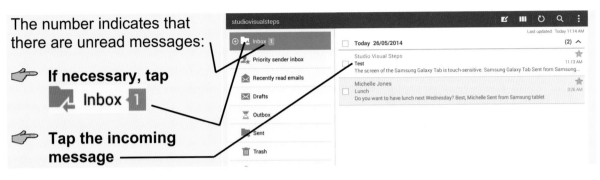

☞ **If necessary, tap**

☞ **Tap the incoming message**

 **HELP! I do not receive any email.**

If you do not receive the email right away, you need to tap the icon at the top of your screen. You can use this icon to retrieve new email:

☞ **Tap** ↻

You will see the content of the message:

On the right-hand side of the bar on top, you will see additional icons. This is what they indicate:

🔍	Search messages.
↻	Retrieve email.
✍	Open a new email message.
↩	Reply to a message.
→	Forward a message.
🗑	Move a message to the *Trash*.
⫴	Adjust the view.
⋮	Open a menu.

This is how you display the folder list again:

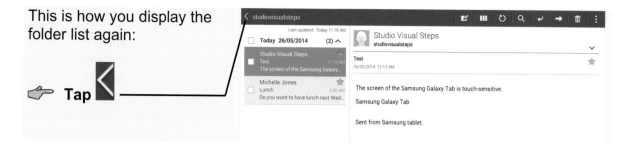

☞ **Tap** ❮

2.4 Deleting an Email

You can delete your test message:

☞ **Check the box** ☑ **by the message**

☞ **Tap** 🗑

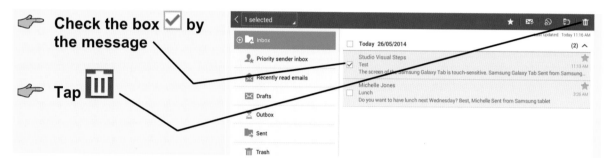

The email has been moved to the *Trash*. You can check to make sure:

☞ **Tap** 🗑 **Trash**

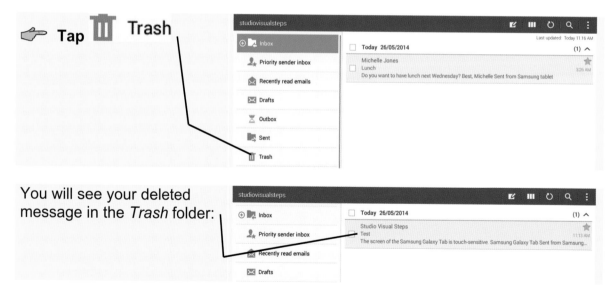

You will see your deleted message in the *Trash* folder:

If you wish, you can also permanently remove the email from the *Trash*:

☞ **Check the box ✓ by the message you want to remove once and for all**

☞ **If you wish, tap 🗑**

☞ **Go back to the home screen** 👣³

☞ **Lock or turn off the Samsung Galaxy Tab, if you wish** 👣¹⁴

In this chapter you have become acquainted with the *Email* app on the Samsung Galaxy Tab. You have learned how to send, receive and delete an email message.

2.5 Background Information

Dictionary

Account
A combination of a user name and a password, that provides access to a specific protected service. A subscription with an Internet service provider is also called an account.

Contacts
A standard app on the Samsung Galaxy Tab, with which you can view and edit your contact data.

Email
A standard app on the Samsung Galaxy Tab, with which you can send and receive email.

Fetch
The traditional way of retrieving new email messages. You open your mail program and connect to the mail server. You can set the program to automatically check for new messages at regular intervals, when the program is opened.

Gmail
A free email service offered by the manufacturers of the well-known *Google* search engine. An app with which you can send and receive the *Gmail* email messages is also called *Gmail*.

Inbox
A folder in which you can view the messages you have received.

Predictive text
A function that displays suggestions for the word you are currently typing.

Push
If *push* is set for your email, and is supported by your Internet service provider, the mail server will immediately send new email messages to your email program, right after they have been received. Even if your email program has not been opened and your Tab is locked.

Signature
A standard salutation that is inserted below all your outgoing email.

Trash
A folder that contains the deleted messages. Once you deleted a message from the *Trash*, the message is permanently deleted.

Source: User manual Samsung Galaxy Tab and Gmail

2.6 Tips

💡 Tip
Add a signature to the messages you send
You can insert a standard text below every email you send. For example, a standard salutation, or your name and address. This text is called your *signature*. This is how you add a signature in the *Email* app:

☞ Tap

☞ If necessary, drag upwards across the menu

☞ Tap **Settings**

☞ Tap your email account

☞ Tap **Signature**

👉 Delete the text ✂️31

⌨️ Type your signature

☞ Tap **Done**

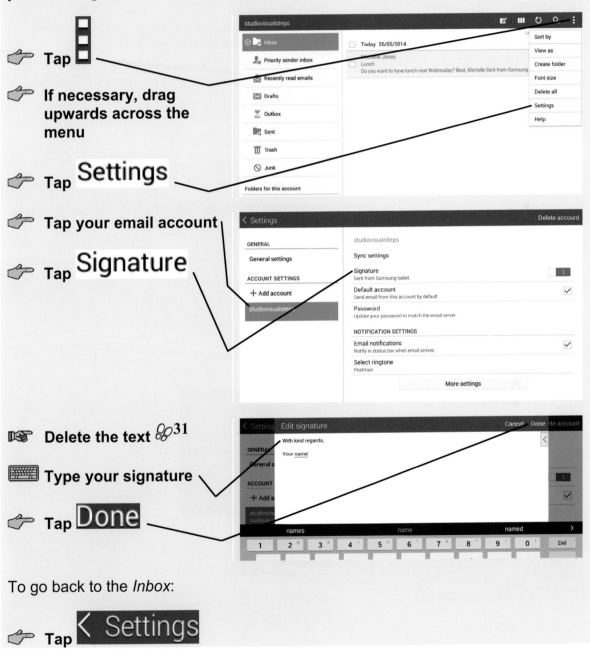

To go back to the *Inbox*:

☞ Tap **< Settings**

💡 Tip
Gmail
If you use *Gmail* you can also use the *Gmail* app, instead of the *Email* app. This app has been especially developed for use with *Google Mail* accounts. It works in a very similar way as the *Email* app.

💡 Tip
Move an email to another folder
You can move email messages to other folders. If you are using an email address ending in @gmail.com, you can create new folders on your Tab. Some email providers, however, will not allow you to create new folders on your Tab. But if you have your email account set up as an IMAP account, and have created folders on your computer, for example, you will see these folders on your Tab. In that case you may also be able to create new folders on your Tab. This is how you create a folder in the *Email* app:

☞ **Open an email message** 🐾*32*

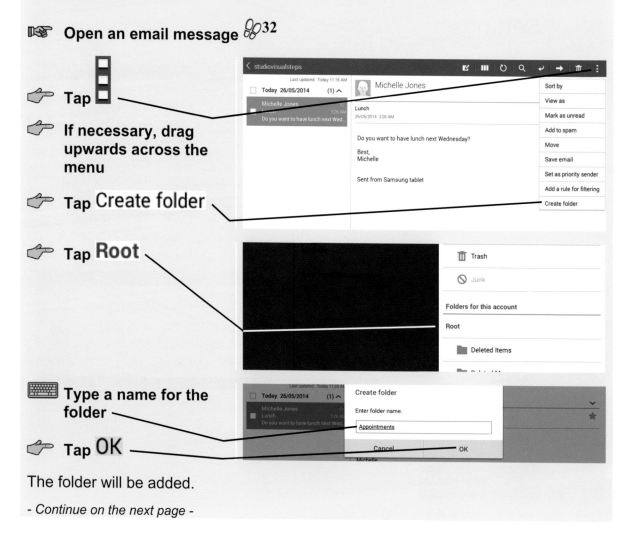

☞ **Tap** ▤

☞ **If necessary, drag upwards across the menu**

☞ **Tap** Create folder

☞ **Tap** Root

⌨ **Type a name for the folder**

☞ **Tap** OK

The folder will be added.

- Continue on the next page -

This is how you move an email message to another folder:

☞ **If necessary, open an email message** 👣**32**

☞ **Tap** ▣

☞ **Tap Move**

☞ **Tap the desired folder**

💡 **Tip**

Push or fetch
If you also use an email program on your computer, you will be used to retrieving your email with the *fetch* option. You open your email program and connect to the mail server, in order to get new messages. You can set the program to automatically check for new messages at regular intervals, once the program has been opened.

Email works with the *push* technology. New email messages are immediately sent to the *Email* app, right after they have been received by the mail server. Even if the *Email* app has not been opened and your Samsung Galaxy Tab is locked. The only time you will not receive any email, is when your Samsung Galaxy Tab has been completely turned off.
While you were setting up the *Email* app, you have seen a screen with a message about your email being synchronized every fifteen minutes. If you want to change this, you can do it in the window where you view the synchronization settings for *Email*. You can practice doing this at the end of this *Tip*.

Please note: if you connect to the Internet through a mobile network and you do not have a subscription that offers unlimited data traffic at a fixed rate, it is better to disable the automatic synchronization function of the *Email* app. If this is the case, you will need to pay for the amount of data you use. If you receive email messages with large attachments on your Samsung Galaxy Tab, you may incur additional data fees. You can manually synchronize your email account the next time you are connected with a Wi-Fi network.

- Continue on the next page -

This is how you view the synchronization settings for *Email*:

☞ **Open the *Email* app** 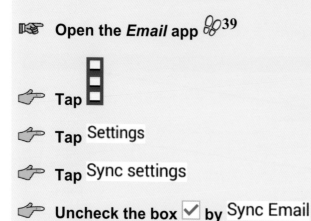**39**

👉 **Tap**

👉 **Tap** Settings

👉 **Tap** Sync settings

👉 **Uncheck the box** ☑ **by** Sync Email

Now your email will no longer be automatically synchronized. You can enable or disable this setting manually with the *Email* app:

👉 **Tap**

💡 **Tip**

Disable predictive text

The *Predictive text* function may sometimes lead to unwanted corrections. The dictionary will not recognize all the words you type, and will still try to come up with suggestions. If you make an occasional typing error, this can lead to rather strange corrections, which you may have accepted without knowing it, by typing a period, comma or a blank space. You can disable the *Predictive text* function if you prefer:

☞ **Open the *Settings* app** **5**

👉 **Tap** Controls

👉 **Tap**
Ⓐ Language and input

👉 **By** Samsung keyboard ,

tap ⚙

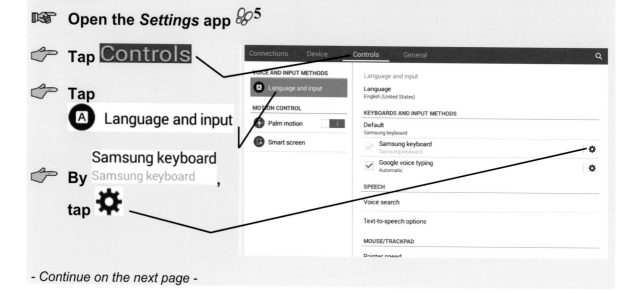

- Continue on the next page -

By the predictive text item you will see a green  (on) or grey/blue (off) icon:

‹ Samsung keyboard settings	
INPUT LANGUAGES	
English(US)	
+ Select input languages	
SMART TYPING	
Predictive text	▮
Auto replacement Complete or replace the word you are typing with the most probable word when you tap the space bar or a punctuation mark.	▮
Auto capitalization Automatically capitalize the first letter of each sentence.	✓
Auto spacing Automatically insert spaces between words.	✓
Auto punctuate Automatically insert a full stop by tapping the space bar twice.	☐
KEYBOARD SWIPE	
None	◉
Continuous input	○

If you click beside the icon, the icon will slide away and you can turn the function on or off.

☞ **Tap beside the icon, if you wish**

☞ **Go back to the home screen** ✂³

If the *Predictive text* function has been turned off, you will no longer see word suggestions as you type.

💡 **Tip**

Create a Samsung account
With a Samsung account you will get access to various online services offered by Samsung. If you would like to create a Samsung account:

☞ **Open the *Settings* app** ✂⁵

☞ **If necessary, tap** General

☞ **If necessary, tap** + Add account

☞ **Tap** Ⓢ Samsung account

Please note: you may need to install some updates first. In order to do this, you need to follow the instructions on the screens.

- Continue on the next page -

If you do not yet have an account:

☞ **Tap**
Create account

You will be asked to enter some information:

☞ **Enter the required data**

Once the data has been entered correctly, you can sign up:

☞ **Tap** Sign up

Agree to the terms:

☞ **If necessary, check the boxes** ✓ **by**
I accept all the terms abov
I acknowledge that my inf
and
I have read and agree wit

☞ **Tap** Agree

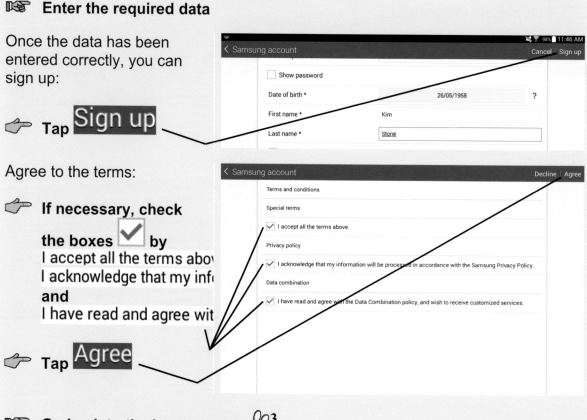

☞ **Go back to the home screen** 🦶³

You have been sent an email, in order to verify your email address. You need to read this email message within 30 days, and open the link in this message.

☞ **Open the email message sent by Samsung in your email program, on your Tab or on your computer**

☞ **Follow the instructions in the email**

3. Surfing with Your Tablet

In this chapter you will learn more about the *Internet* app. This is the web browser application that comes with your Samsung Galaxy Tab. You can use this app to surf the Internet on your tablet. If you are used to surfing the Internet on your computer, you will notice that surfing is just as easy on the Samsung Galaxy Tab. The main difference is that you do not need to use a mouse with your Tab. You can surf by using touch gestures on the screen.

You will learn how to open a web page and you will get acquainted with other touch gestures that allow you to zoom in, zoom out and scroll. We will also explain how to open links (also called hyperlinks) and work with saved web pages.

You can use the *Internet* app to open multiple web pages at once. As you work through this chapter you will see how easy it is to switch between these open pages.

While you are surfing you may see a need to adjust a particular setting. Your Samsung Galaxy Tab is able to execute multiple tasks at once, so you can do this at any time. You can switch from one app to another, recently used app. All of these things are explained in this chapter.

In this chapter you will learn how to:

- open the *Internet* app;
- open a web page;
- zoom in and zoom out;
- scroll;
- open a link on a web page;
- open a link in a new tab;
- switch between open web pages;
- add a bookmark;
- search;
- switch between recently used apps.

➥ Please note:

While you are using your Tab, you may see some screens that provide additional information about the operation of an app or the keyboard. You can read the information and tap **Done** or OK afterwards.

3.1 Opening the Internet App

This is how you open *Internet*, the app that lets you surf the Internet:

☞ **Unlock or turn on the Samsung Galaxy Tab**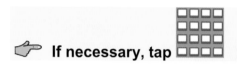

You can open the *Internet* app:

☞ **If necessary, tap**

☞ **Tap Internet**

The icon for this app may
already be shown on the
home screen of your own
Tab.

You will see the app's start
screen:

Most visited

Google

Google

3.2 Opening a Web Page

In order to type a web address, you need to display the onscreen keyboard:

☞ **Tap the address bar**

The onscreen keyboard will appear at the bottom of the screen.

To practice typing an address, you will use the Visual Steps website:

Type: www.

Right away, you will see all kinds of suggestions:

The more letters you type for this address, the more specific the suggestions will become.

Type: visualsteps.com

When you have finished typing:

☞ **Tap** Go

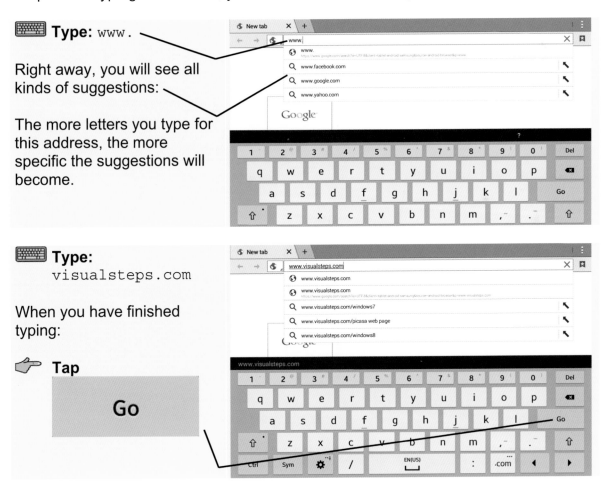

💡 **Tip**

Use a suggestion

Of course, you can also tap 🌐 www.visualsteps.com in the suggestions list.

You will see the Visual Steps website:

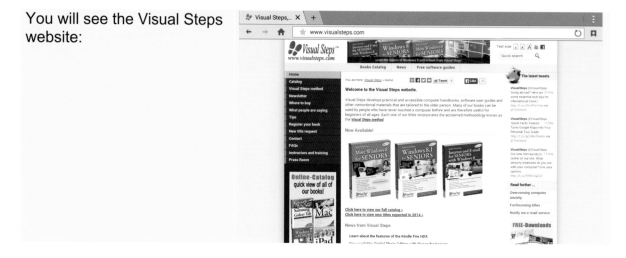

3.3 Zooming In and Out

If you think the letters and images on a website are too small, you can zoom in. This is done by double-tapping. You tap the desired location twice, in rapid succession:

👉 **Double-tap the menu on the left-hand side**

✚ HELP! A different web page is opened.

If you do not succeed at double-tapping right away, another window may be opened.

In that case, you can tap ⬅ in the top left-hand side of the screen and try again. You can also practice double-tapping on a blank section of the screen.

Now you will see that the size of the web page has increased:

☞ **Double-tap the menu once more**

The screen will zoom out again and display the regular view. There is yet another way of zooming in. You will need to use two fingers to do this:

☞ **Spread your thumb and index finger across the screen**

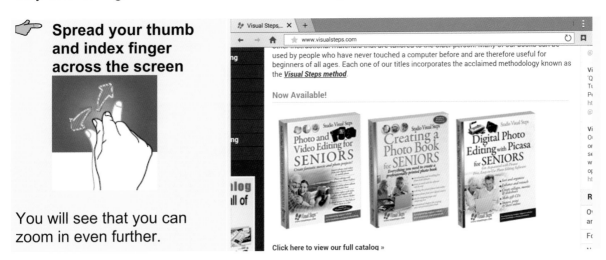

You will see that you can zoom in even further.

You can zoom out again by doing the opposite (pinching your fingers together):

☞ **Move your thumb and index finger towards each other across the screen**

Go back to the regular view:

☞ **Double-tap the page**

You will see the regular view again:

3.4 Scrolling

When you scroll a web page it means you are moving the text and images that appear on the web page across your screen. In this way you can view the full content of a web page. On your Samsung Galaxy Tab you use your fingers to scroll a page:

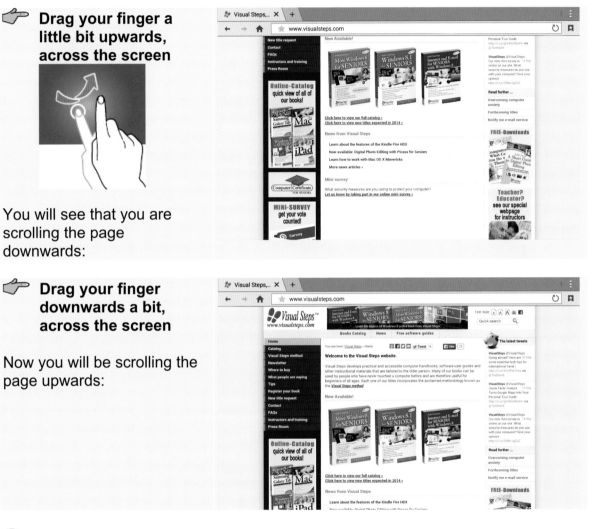

☞ **Drag your finger a little bit upwards, across the screen**

You will see that you are scrolling the page downwards:

☞ **Drag your finger downwards a bit, across the screen**

Now you will be scrolling the page upwards:

💡 **Tip**

Scrolling sideways
On a wide web page you can also scroll sideways by moving your finger across the screen from right to left or from left to right.

If you want to quickly scroll through a long page, you can use a swiping (flicking) gesture:

☞ **Quickly swipe your finger upwards across the screen**

You will rapidly scroll down the page:

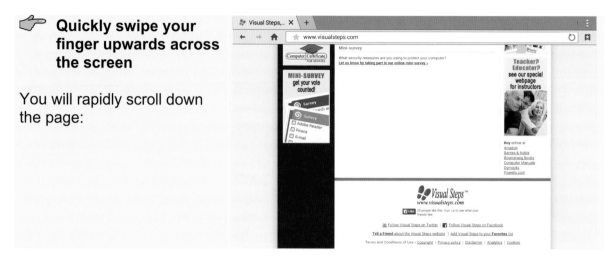

💡 **Tip**

Move in different directions
You can also quickly scroll upwards, to the left, or to the right, if you make the swiping gesture in a different direction.

This is how you quickly go to the top of the page:

☞ **Quickly swipe your finger downwards across the screen**

You will see the top of the web page again:

3.5 Opening a Link on a Web Page

If a page contains a link (also called hyperlink), you can open it by tapping the link.
Just try it:

A part of the screen may be enlarged:

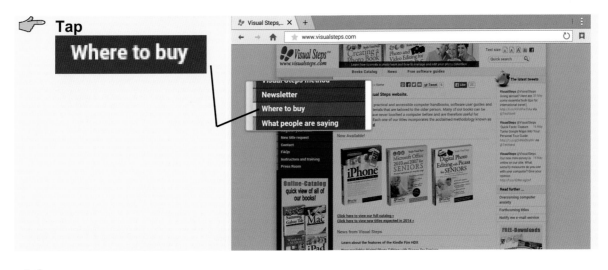

HELP! Tapping the link does not work.

If you find it hard to tap the right link, you can zoom in first. The links will be
displayed much larger, and tapping a link will become easier.

Here you can see the web page about where to find the Visual Steps books:

3.6 Opening a Link in a New Tab

You can also open a link in a new tab:

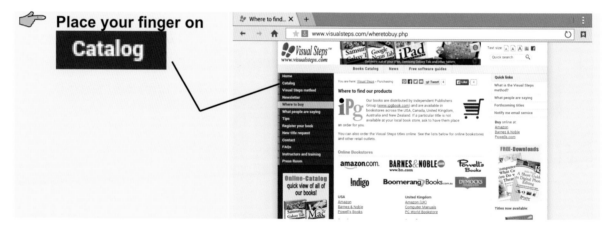

☞ **Place your finger on**
Catalog

After a while you will see a new menu:

☞ **Tap**
Open in new tab

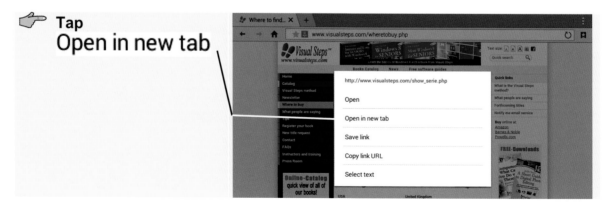

The linked page will be opened in a new tab:

You will see the page with the Visual Steps catalog:

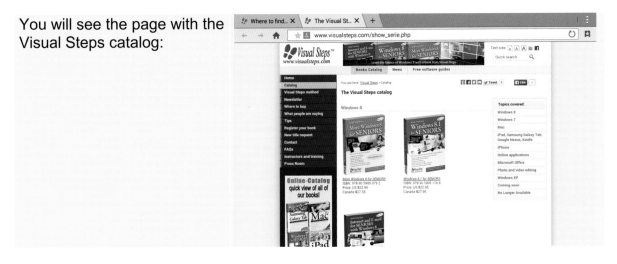

This is how you go back to the first tab:

Once more, you will see the Where to find our products web page.

☞ **Go to the second tab** 🐾**15**

This is how you close an open tab:

Once again, you will see the Visual Steps Where to find our products web page:

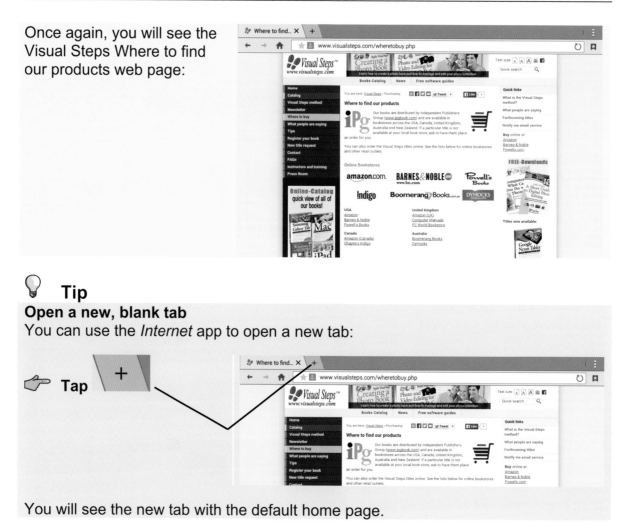

Tip

Open a new, blank tab
You can use the *Internet* app to open a new tab:

Tap

You will see the new tab with the default home page.

3.7 Go to a Previous or Next Page

You can go back to the web page you previously visited. You do that like this:

Tap

You will see the Visual Steps home page again. You can also go to the next page.

You can use the ➡ button to do this, but for now this will not be necessary.

3.8 Adding a Bookmark

If you want to visit a particular web page in the future, you can add a bookmark for it. A bookmark is the address of a website that has been saved so you can access the web site easier and faster later on. If you set a bookmark, you will not need to type the full web address every time you want to visit the page. Here is how to add a bookmark for a web page that is already open:

☞ **Tap** ⭐

You will see thumbnails for the bookmarked websites in the Bookmarks overview:

☞ **Tap** ➕

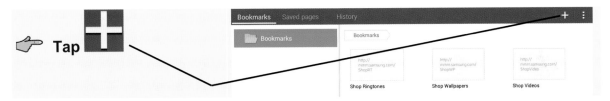

In the *Add bookmark* window you can type an easily identifiable name for the web page, if you wish. For now this will not be necessary. Save the bookmark:

⌨ **Type:** Visual Steps

☞ **Tap** **Save**

The web page has been added to your bookmarks:

☞ **If necessary, drag the screen upwards**

You will see a new thumbnail for the bookmark in the overview:

Samsung has already added a number of useful bookmarks for you, such as the tablet's user manual:

☞ **Tap**

http://
www.google.com/

Google
(Google)

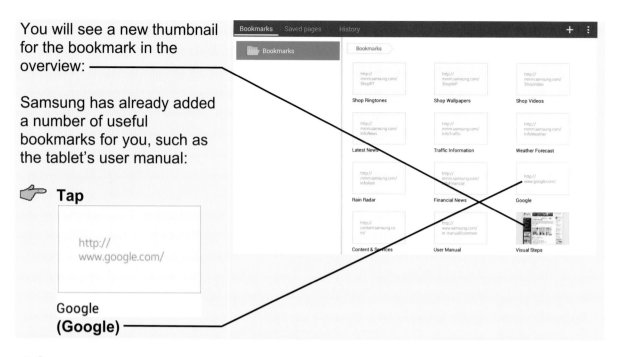

🩹 **HELP! I do not see this bookmark.**

If you do not see the bookmark for the user manual, just tap a different bookmark.

You will see the *Google* website:

Go back to the Visual Steps web page:

☞ **Tap** ⭐

☞ **If necessary, drag the screen upwards**

☞ **Tap**

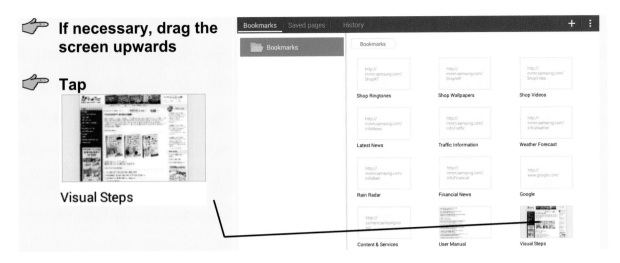

Visual Steps

You will see the Visual Steps web page again.

3.9 Searching

The *Internet* app uses the *Google* search engine. You may already be familiar with using a search box to enter your search terms or phrases, like you do in other Internet browsers installed on your computer. On the Tab it works in a similar fashion:

☞ **Tap the address bar**

The address bar is replaced by the search box, and the onscreen keyboard appears. Now you can enter your keywords:

⌨ **Type:** Samsung Galaxy Tab sleeve

As you type, you will see all sorts of suggestions for your keywords:

If you want to use one of these suggestions, you just tap it. For now this will not be necessary.

In this example you will use the keywords that you typed:

☞ **Tap** **Go**

Here you see the search results:

To view one of these results, you need to tap the link. For now this will not be necessary.

3.10 Switching between Recently Used Apps

You can quickly switch between the apps you have recently used. Just try it:

☞ **Press the Recent apps button**

A menu with recently used apps will appear:

You may see different apps than the ones shown in this example:

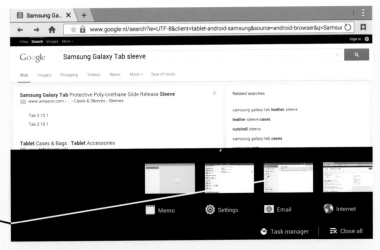

👉 **For example, tap**

If you want to scroll through the list, just drag the screen, from right to left or from left to right.

You will see the *Email* app:

👉 **Press the Recent apps button** 🔲

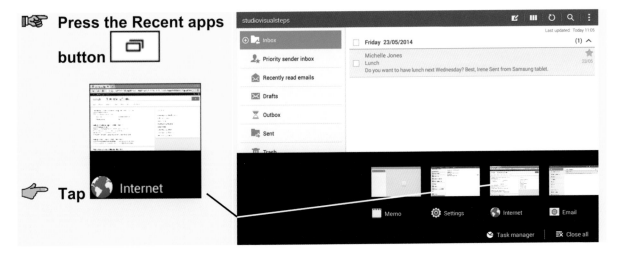

👉 **Tap** 🌐 **Internet**

Now you will see the *Internet* app again.

You can also switch between apps using the multi window:

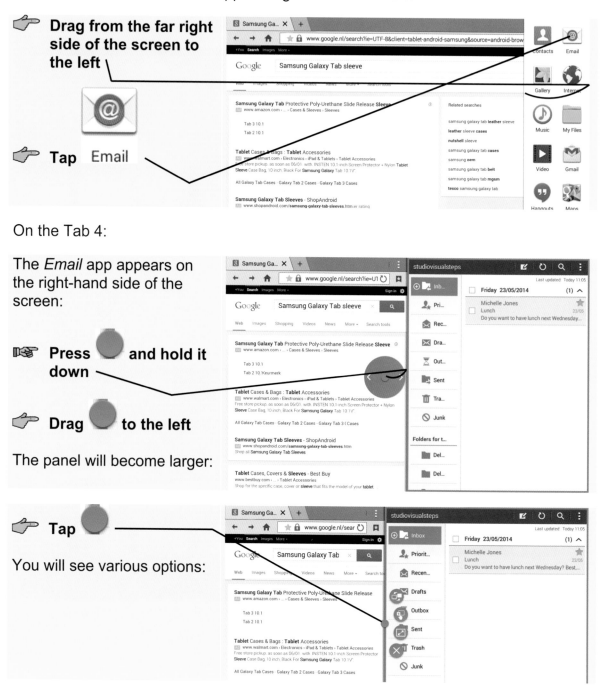

Drag from the far right side of the screen to the left

Tap Email

On the Tab 4:

The *Email* app appears on the right-hand side of the screen:

Press and hold it **down**

Drag to the left

The panel will become larger:

Tap

You will see various options:

Tap  to switch the position of the panel from left to right, and the other way round.

Tap to drag text, pictures or links to the other panel.

Tap to display the panel on a full screen.

Tap to close the panel.

☞ **Tap** ✕

On the TabPro and NotePro, the app will appear in a new window:

You can hide (minimize) this window temporarily:

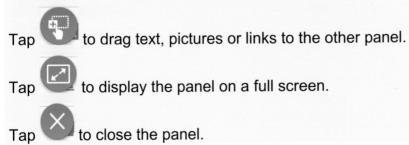

☞ **Tap** ▬

Now you will see the screen with the search results again. To display the *Email* app again:

☞ **Tap** ▬

You will see the window of the *Email* app:

You can also maximize the
window, by using the

button 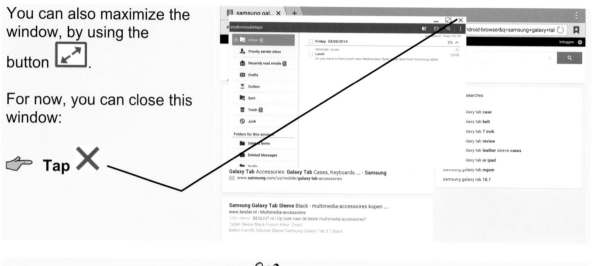.

For now, you can close this
window:

👉 **Tap** ✕

☞ **Go back to the home screen** 👣³

☞ **Lock or turn off the Samsung Galaxy Tab, if you wish** 👣¹⁴

In this chapter you have learned how to work with the *Internet* app. Furthermore, you
have learned how to use new touch gestures for zooming in and out and scrolling
through web pages.

3.11 Background Information

Dictionary

Bookmark	A reference to a web address stored in a list that allows quick and easy access to a web page later on.
Google	*Google* is mainly known for its search engine, but offers other services as well, such as *Google Maps* and *Gmail*.
Home page	The web page that is displayed when you open the *Internet* app, or a new tab.
Hyperlink	Another name for a link.
Link	A link is a navigation method on a web page that automatically leads the user to the information when it is tapped. It may be represented as text, an image, a button or an icon. A link is also called a hyperlink.
Scroll	Moving a web page across the screen, upwards, downwards, to the left or to the right. On the Samsung Galaxy Tab you use touch gestures to accomplish this.
Stored pages	You can store web pages in this list, and read them later on, even when you do not have an Internet connection. You can only store the page that was displayed at the time, not the entire website. If you want to view multiple web pages offline, you will need to store these pages separately.
Zoom in	Take a closer look at an item, the letters and images will be enlarged.
Zoom out	View an item from a greater distance, the letters and images will become smaller.

Source: User manual Samsung Galaxy Tab, Wikipedia

3.12 Tips

♀ Tip

Quickly type a web address
The onscreen keyboard appears when you tap the address bar. On the onscreen
keyboard you will see the   **www·**   key. You can use this key to quickly type the
first part of the web address.

As soon as you type the rest of the web address, the   **·com**   will be displayed.
You can use the same key to type other kinds of extensions, such as .net, .org, .edu,
and .gov.

☞ **Place your finger on the   ·com   key**

You will see a small window with various extensions:

☞ **Move your finger from   ·com   to the extension you want to use**

Please note: if you release the key beforehand, the small window will disappear.

☞ **Release the key**

The extension will appear in the address bar.

♀ Tip

Delete a bookmark
If you no longer want to use a bookmark, you can delete it like this:

☞ **Tap**

- Continue on the next page -

👉 **If necessary, drag your finger upwards across the screen**

👉 **Place your finger on the bookmark you want to delete**

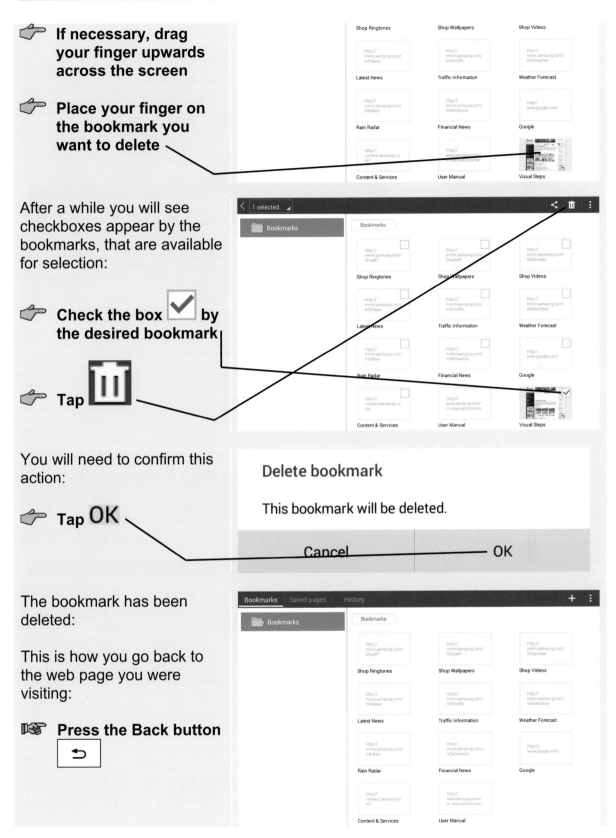

After a while you will see checkboxes appear by the bookmarks, that are available for selection:

👉 **Check the box ✅ by the desired bookmark**

👉 **Tap** 🗑

You will need to confirm this action:

👉 **Tap OK**

Delete bookmark

This bookmark will be deleted.

Cancel — OK

The bookmark has been deleted:

This is how you go back to the web page you were visiting:

👉 **Press the Back button** �

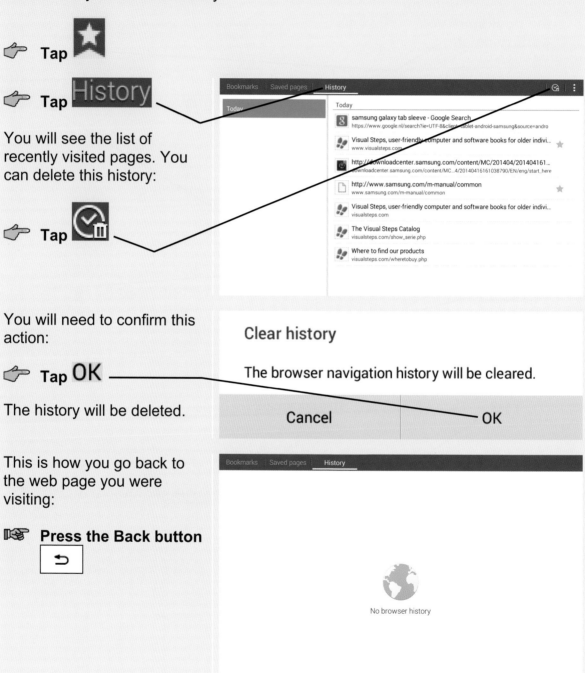

Tip

View and delete history

The browser history contains all the websites you have recently visited.
This is how you view the history:

☞ **Tap** ⭐

☞ **Tap** History

You will see the list of
recently visited pages. You
can delete this history:

☞ **Tap**

You will need to confirm this
action:

☞ **Tap** OK

The history will be deleted.

This is how you go back to
the web page you were
visiting:

☞ **Press the Back button**
🔙

Bookmarks | Saved pages | History

Today

Today

🔍 samsung galaxy tab sleeve - Google Search
https://www.google.nl/search?ie=UTF-8&client=tablet-android-samsung&source=andro

👣 Visual Steps, user-friendly computer and software books for older indivi... ⭐
www.visualsteps.com

📄 http://downloadcenter.samsung.com/content/MC/201404/201404161...
downloadcenter.samsung.com/content/MC...4/20140416161038790/EN/eng/start_here

📄 http://www.samsung.com/m-manual/common ⭐
www.samsung.com/m-manual/common

👣 Visual Steps, user-friendly computer and software books for older indivi...
visualsteps.com

👣 The Visual Steps Catalog
visualsteps.com/show_serie.php

👣 Where to find our products
visualsteps.com/wheretobuy.php

Clear history

The browser navigation history will be cleared.

Cancel	OK

Bookmarks | Saved pages | History

🌐

No browser history

💡 Tip

Set a home page

You can set your favorite website as the home page for your web browser. After you have opened the web page, this is what you do:

👉 **Tap** ⫶

👉 **Drag upwards across the menu**

👉 **Tap Settings**

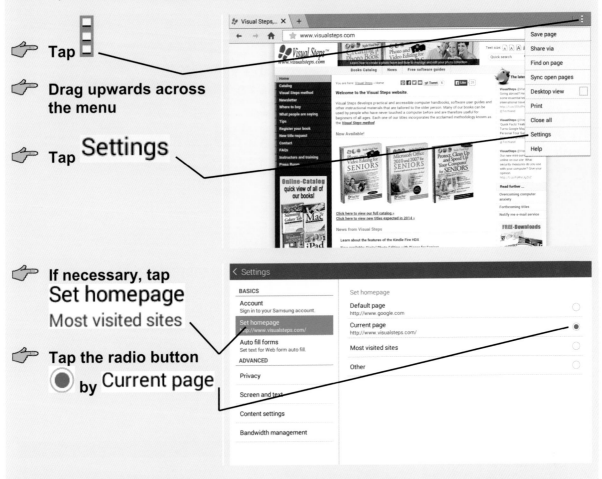

👉 **If necessary, tap Set homepage Most visited sites**

👉 **Tap the radio button ⊙ by Current page**

The home page has been added. From now on, you will see your favorite website whenever you open a new tab. To save the changes:

👉 **Tap**

💡 Tip

Store pages for offline reading

In the *Internet* app you can store web pages to view and read later on, for example, when you do not have a Wi-Fi connection. This is how you store a web page:

☞ Tap

☞ Tap **Save page**

The page will be added to the saved pages.

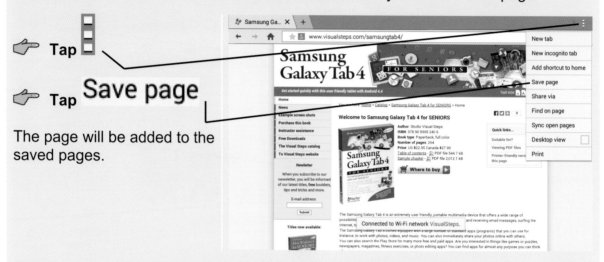

Please note: the page that was on the screen when you tapped the save command is the only page that will be stored, the rest of the website will not be saved. If you want to view multiple pages of a website offline, you will need to save these pages separately.

To open a web page you have previously saved:

☞ Tap

☞ Tap **Saved pages**

☞ **Tap the desired web page**

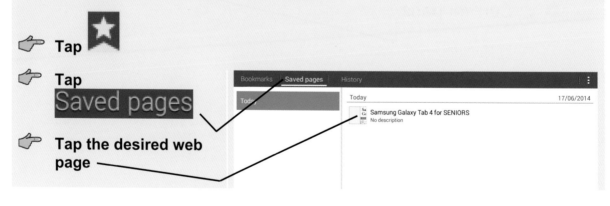

4. Managing Your Contacts, Calendar, and Widgets

Your Samsung Galaxy Tab contains a number of other standard apps besides *Email* and *Internet*. For example, you can use the *Contacts* app to manage your contacts. You can add contacts and synchronize them with the contacts list on your computer. If you choose this option, the contacts on your Tab and on your computer will become the same. You can edit or delete the contacts contained in the list directly with your Samsung Galaxy Tab.

In the *S Planner* app (also called *Calendar* app) you can keep track of your appointments and other activities. If you already keep a calendar in *Outlook*, you can transfer this calendar to your Samsung Galaxy Tab. You can also add, edit, and delete events directly on the Tab.

Along with these handy apps, your tablet also features a number of standard widgets. These are small programs that offer information from the Internet or provide other useful functions. In this chapter you will find out more about them.

In this chapter you will learn how to:

- add contacts in the *Contacts* app;
- search for contacts;
- edit and delete contacts;
- add calendar items in the *S Planner* app;
- edit and delete calendar items;
- work with widgets.

Please note:

While you are using your Tab, you may see some screens that provide additional information about the operation of an app or the keyboard. You can read the information and tap **Done** or **OK** afterwards.

4.1 Adding a Contact

Open the *Contacts* app from the list of all apps, or from the home screen:

☞ **Unlock or turn on the Samsung Galaxy Tab** $\mathcal{QO}$ **9**

☞ **If necessary, tap**

☞ **Tap Contacts**

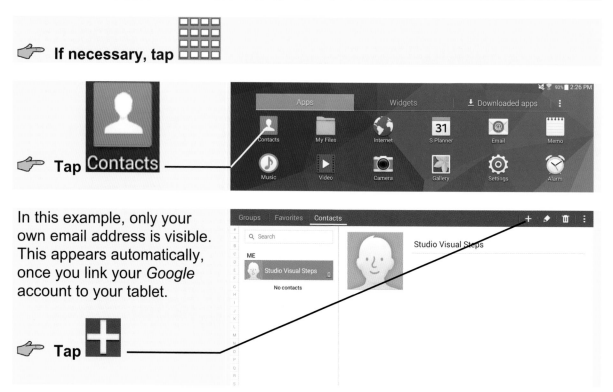

In this example, only your own email address is visible. This appears automatically, once you link your *Google* account to your tablet.

☞ **Tap**

You will be asked where you want to save the new contact. You can choose between the SIM card (on the Samsung Galaxy Tab Wi-Fi + 3G/4G), your *Google* account, your Samsung account, or on this device only. In this example the *Google* account will be chosen. In this way you can automatically synchronize your contacts with your computer and other devices, if you wish.

☞ **Tap**

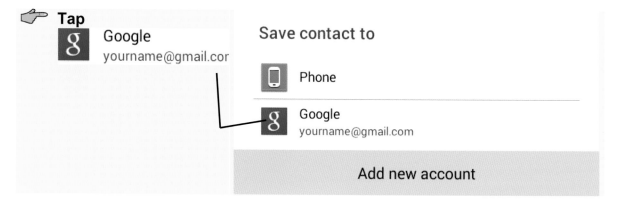

You may see this message:

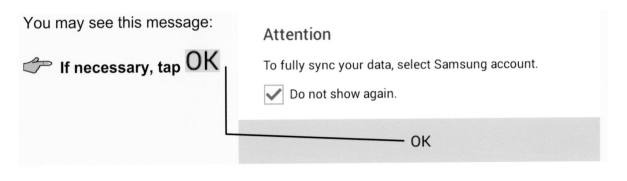

☞ **If necessary, tap OK**

Attention

To fully sync your data, select Samsung account.

☑ Do not show again.

OK

💡 **Tip**

Contacts will be synchronized
If you have already added contacts to your *Google* account on another device, such as a cell phone, they will be synchronized automatically to your Samsung Galaxy Tab when you are connected to the Internet.

You will see the window where you can add a new contact:

☞ **Tap** ⌄

In this example we will add a fictitious contact. You can type the actual data for a friend or family member, if you wish. You do this by using the onscreen keyboard:

☞ **Tap** First name

⌨ **Type your contact's first name**

☞ **Tap** Last name

⌨ **Type your contact's last name**

You can choose which fields you want to fill in. You also can reduce the size of the name box like this:

☞ **Tap** ⋀

💡 **Tip**
Even faster
If you only use the First name and Last name boxes, you really do not need to open the box. You can just type the full name (for example: Michael Clayton) directly into the Name box.

☞ **Tap** Phone number

⌨ **Type your contact's mobile phone number**

Add a second line for a phone number:

☞ **Tap** +

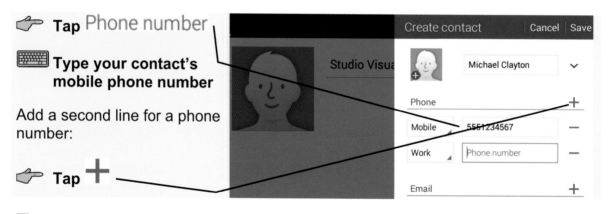

➦ **Please note:**
If you type a phone number, sometimes blank spaces will be added automatically and sometimes they will not. But when you need to use the phone number it doesn't matter if there are blank spaces or not.

By default, the label for the next phone number field is │ Work ◢ │. You can change this label yourself. You can turn it into a home phone number, for instance:

☞ **Tap** │ Work ◢ │

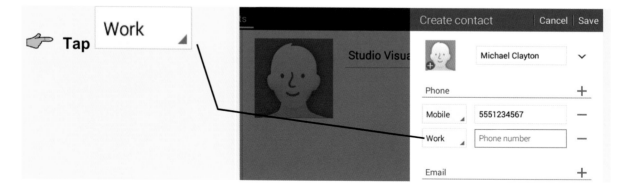

You will see a list of available labels:

☞ **Tap** Home

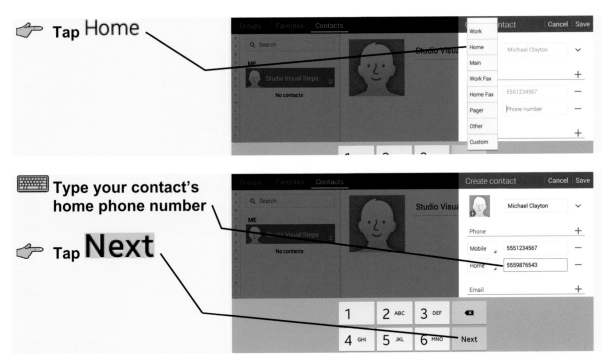

⌨ **Type your contact's home phone number**

☞ **Tap** Next

⌨ **Type your contact's email address**

💡 **Tip**

Change the label
You can also change the label for an email address, from home to work, for example.

☞ **Tap**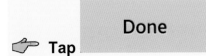

Now you can add your contact's home address. You will need to add a field first:

☞ **If necessary, drag the page upwards**

☞ **Tap**
Add another field

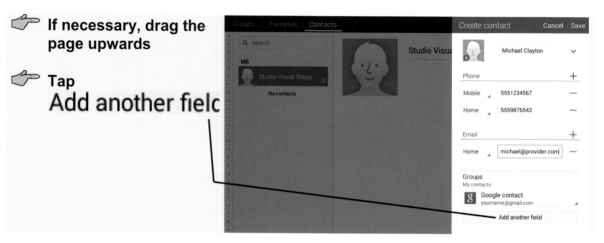

In the next window:

☞ **Check the box** ✓ **by Address**

☞ **Tap OK**

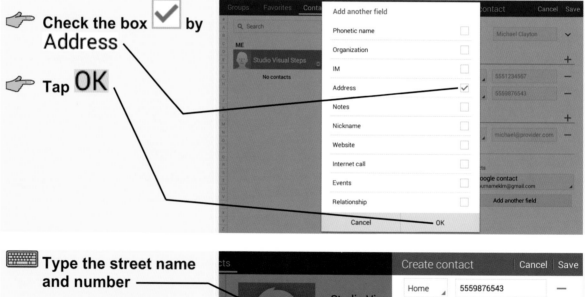

⌨ **Type the street name and number**

☞ **Drag the window upwards, if needed**

Now you add the zip (postal) code and city:

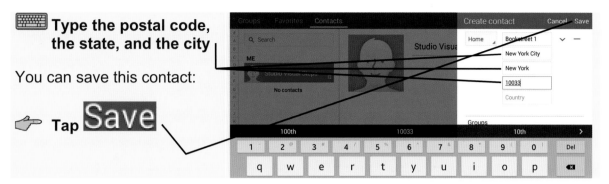

Type the postal code, the state, and the city

You can save this contact:

☞ **Tap** Save

You will see a message about your contact having multiple phone numbers. You can select one of these numbers as the default phone number:

☞ **Tap** OK

☞ **Tap the radio button**

⊙ **by the number you want to set as a default**

☞ **Tap** Done

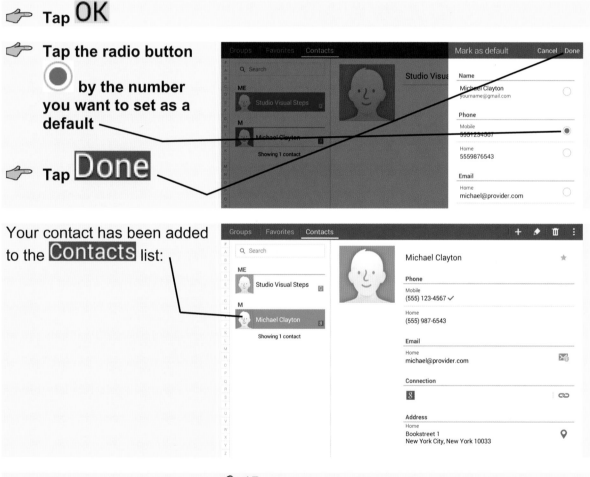

Your contact has been added to the Contacts list:

☞ **Add four more contacts** ✂️**17**

You may have some difficulty reading all the names in your contact list. If you widen the name box a little, it is easier to read the full names:

☞ **Place your finger on the borderline between the list and the contact data**

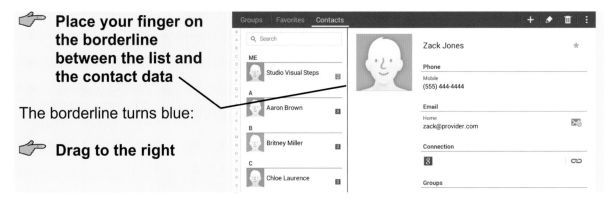

The borderline turns blue:

☞ **Drag to the right**

Now you can read even the longer names. If you want to make the box a bit smaller again, just drag the line a little to the left.

4.2 Editing a Contact

After you have added all your contacts, you may want to edit the data later on. For example, in order to change an address, or add a new phone number. This is how you open a contact for editing:

☞ **Tap the desired contact**

☞ **Tap**

This is how you edit the phone number, for example:

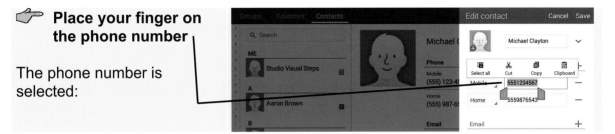

☞ **Place your finger on the phone number**

The phone number is selected:

You can type the new phone number right away:

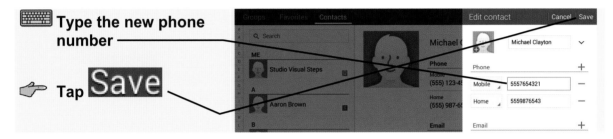

⌨ **Type the new phone number**

☞ **Tap** **Save**

4.3 Finding a Contact

If you have added a lot of contacts to the *Contacts* app, it may be difficult to quickly find the right contact. Fortunately, the app contains a handy search function:

☞ **Tap** 🔍 Search

⌨ **Type the first letter of the first or last name**

In this example, a contact is found whose first name starts with the letter z:

☞ **Tap ✕**

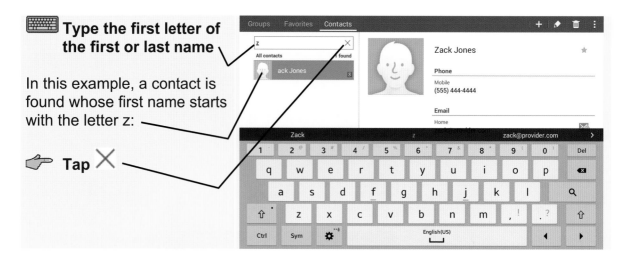

4.4 Deleting a Contact

This is how you delete unnecessary contacts:

☞ **Tap the desired contact**

☞ **Tap** 🗑

You will need to confirm this action:

☞ **Tap OK**

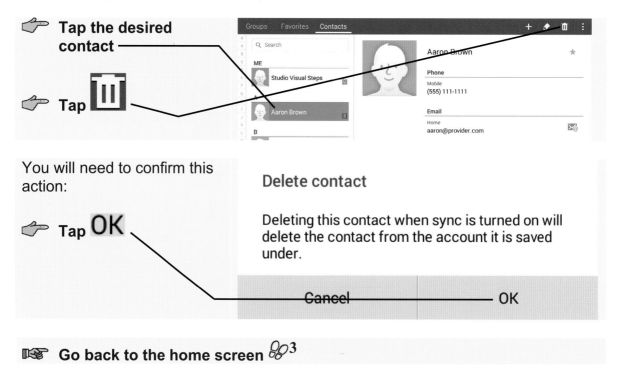

Delete contact

Deleting this contact when sync is turned on will delete the contact from the account it is saved under.

Cancel　　　　　　　　OK

☞ **Go back to the home screen** 👣³

4.5 S Planner

In the *S Planner* you can keep a diary. This is how you open the app:

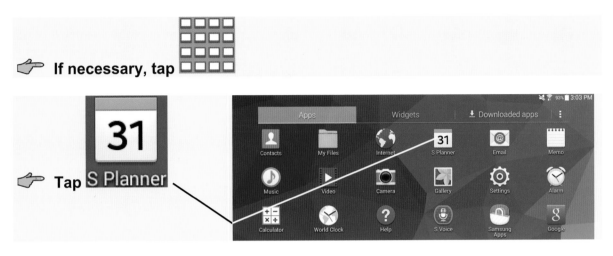

☞ **If necessary, tap**

☞ **Tap** S Planner

The calendar opens with a view of the current month:

At the top you can select a different view: ⎯⎯⎯

If you have selected another date than the current day, you can use the Today button to quickly return to today's events: ⎯⎯⎯

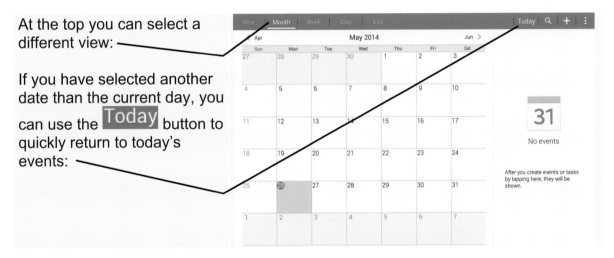

You can change the view per day, week, month, and year. You can view a full week at once, for example:

☞ **Tap** Week

You will see this week's view. You can quickly jump to the next week:

☞ **Swipe the screen from right to left**

You will see the next week.

4.6 Adding an Event to the Calendar

An appointment is called an event in the *S Planner* app. You can practice adding an event to your calendar:

☞ **Tap the desired day, for example, Friday**

In order to add the event:

☞ **Tap**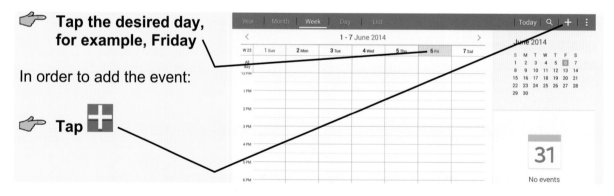

You may see a message regarding the synchronization with *Samsung Kies 3*. Your *Google* calendar will automatically be synchronized with your *Google* account. For now you do not need to change any of these settings.

☞ **If necessary, tap**

You can enter a name for the event:

⌨ **Type a name, for example:** Tennis lesson

You can change the start and end times for the event:

☞ **Tap**

    Fri 06/06/2014 8:00 AM

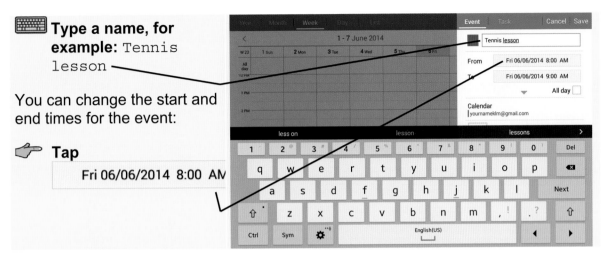

You can adjust the hours and minutes forward or backward with the ⌃ and ⌄ buttons:

☞ **Tap ⌃ or ⌄ until the hours reach**

7

☞ **If necessary, tap**

AM

If the start time is correct:

☞ **Tap Set**

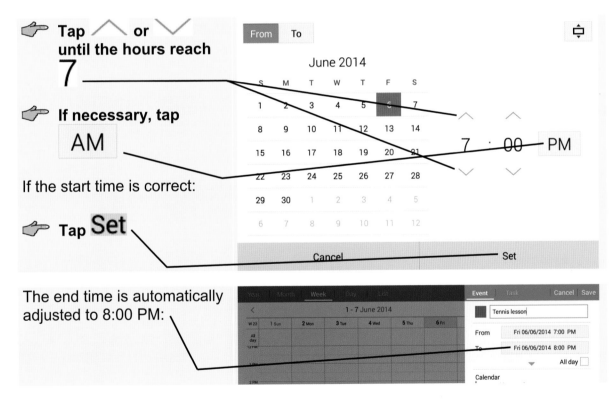

The end time is automatically adjusted to 8:00 PM:

💡 **Tip**

Correct start time
If you add an event by clicking the correct time box at the beginning, the start time will be set correctly right away.

💡 **Tip**

Whole day
If an event lasts all day:

👉 **Check the box** ☑ by All day

You can use even more options in the window where you add an event:

Repeat   Here you can set the event to be repeated with a certain frequency. For instance, every week or every month. By default, the One-time event option has been selected.

Reminder   Here you can set a reminder for the activity by tapping ➕. The reminder will be sent in the form of a notification or an email. You can choose whether you want to be reminded just a couple of minutes before the event starts, or even a couple of hours, or days. By default, the Notification and 15 mins before options have been selected.

You can also enter a location for the event:

👉 **Tap** Location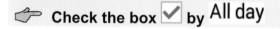

⌨️ **Type a location, for example:** Tennis court

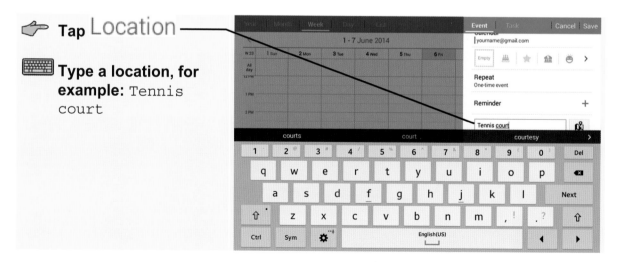

After you have entered all the data concerning the event:

☞ **Tap** Save

☞ **If necessary, swipe the page upwards**

You will see the event on the calendar:

4.7 Editing or Deleting an Event

If an event changes or is canceled, you can edit it like this:

☞ **Tap the event**

☞ **Tap**

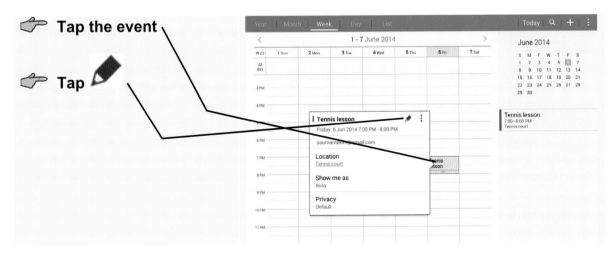

You may see a message about the *Google* calendar not being able to synchronize with *Samsung Kies*:

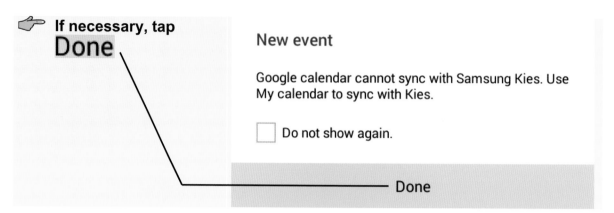

You will see the window again where you had entered the event. For now you do not need to change anything:

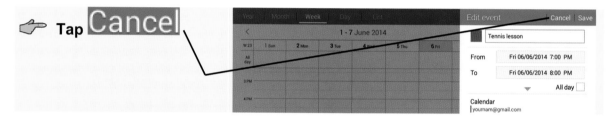

If you want to delete the event, you can do that like this:

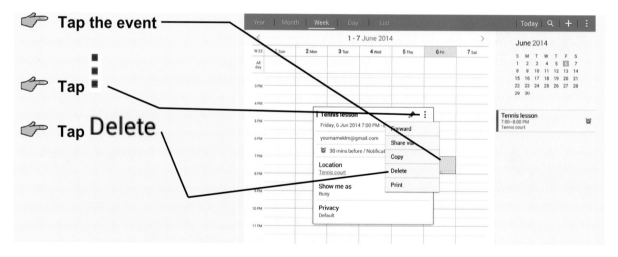

You will need to confirm this action:

☞ **Go back to the home screen** ৪৫³

You have learned to work with the *Contacts* and *S Planner* apps. In the next chapter you will learn how to work with some other apps and learn how to close an app.

4.8 Working with Widgets

The home screen of your Tab contains a number of *widgets*. These are small programs that offer information from the Internet or provide other useful functions. On your other pages, you may see some widgets too, for example, the second or third page:

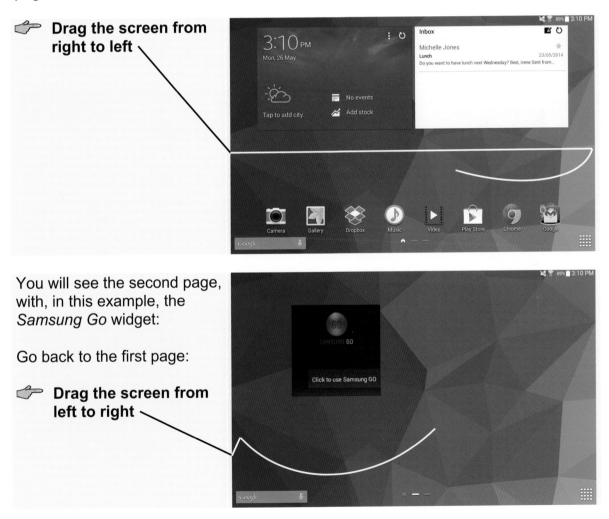

☞ **Drag the screen from right to left**

You will see the second page, with, in this example, the *Samsung Go* widget:

Go back to the first page:

☞ **Drag the screen from left to right**

This is how you use the weather widget, for example:

☞ **Tap** Tap to add city.

The program will probably want to search for your location. Next:

☞ **Tap your current location**

You will see the widget with the current weather forecast appear on your home screen:

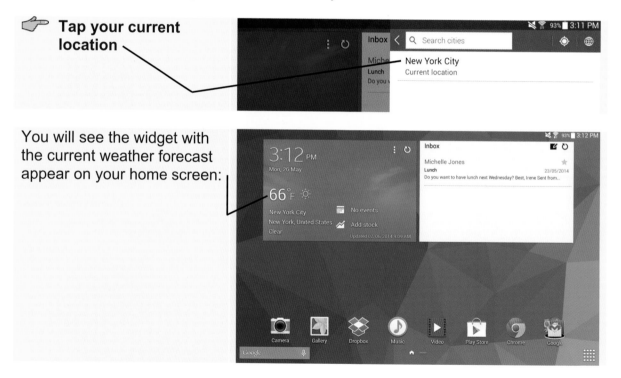

There are several other widgets you can use. Here is how to view them:

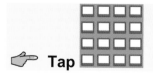

☞ **Tap**

☞ Tap ▐Widgets▌

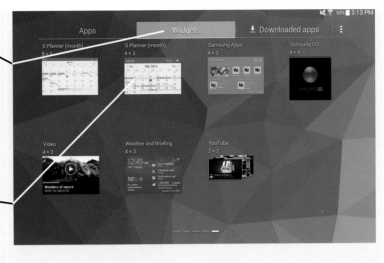

To view more widgets:

☞ **Swipe the screen from right to left**

☞ **Place your finger on a widget**

In this example we have selected the *S Planner (month) 4 x 3* widget. You may not see this widget on your own screen. If that is the case, you can select a different widget.

The Tab suggests placing the app on the first page, but this page is already quite crowded. You can place the widget on the second page:

☞ **Drag to the right-hand edge of the screen**

Now, you can place the widget on the second page:

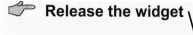 **Release the widget**

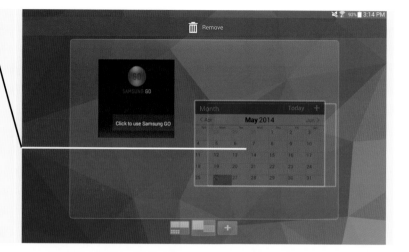

The widget has been placed on the second page:

If you have selected the *S Planner* widget, you will see today's date: ———

If an event has been added, you will see it in the widget:

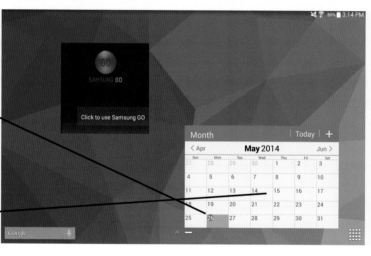

You can also drag a widget to another page:

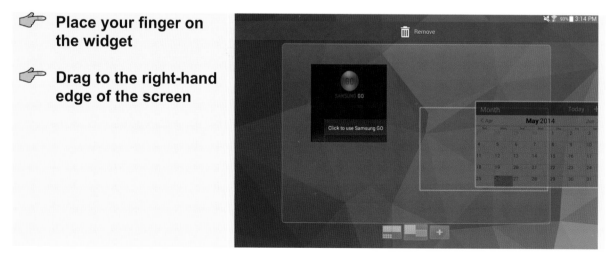 **Place your finger on the widget**

Drag to the right-hand edge of the screen

☞ **Release the widget**

☞ **Place one more widget on the page that is displayed** 🐾³³

This is how you delete a widget if you do not want it to be displayed on the page anymore:

☞ **Place your finger on the widget**

☞ **Drag to**

☞ **Release the widget**

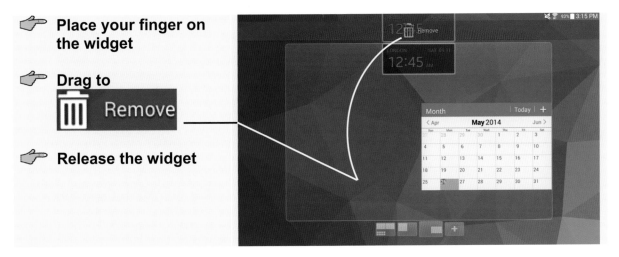

The widget has been removed from the page.

☞ **Go back to the home screen** 🐾³

☞ **Lock or turn off the Samsung Galaxy Tab, if you wish** 🐾¹⁴

In this chapter you have learned to use the *Contacts* and *S Planner* apps. You have also learned how to work with widgets.

4.9 Background Information

Dictionary

Contacts	An app in which you can add and manage contacts.
Event	An appointment in the *S Planner* app.
Field	The box where you enter data for a contact. *First name* and *Postal code* are examples of fields.
Google Calendar	A service offered by *Google*, where you can keep a calendar. You can use your *Google* account for this.
Hangouts	An app with which you can hold video chats through an Internet connection. You can chat with friends who have a *Google* account and use *Google Hangouts* as well.
Label	Name of a field.
Outlook	An email program, part of the *Microsoft Office* suite.
S Planner	An app with which you can keep track of your activities and appointments.
Synchronize	Literally: equalize. Not only can you synchronize your Samsung Galaxy Tab with the content of your *Library* in *Samsung Kies 3*, but you can also synchronize contact data or a calendar.

Source: User manual Samsung Galaxy Tab, Wikipedia

4.10 Tips

  Tip

Add a photo

If you have stored a photo of your contact on your Samsung Galaxy Tab, you can add this photo to his or her contact information. In *Chapter 7 Photos and Video* you can read how to take pictures with your Samsung Galaxy Tab and how to transfer photos to your Tab. This is how you add an existing photo to a contact:

☞ **Open the *Contacts* app** 🐾**19**

☞ **Tap the desired contact**

☞ **Tap** ✏️

☞ **Tap** ➕

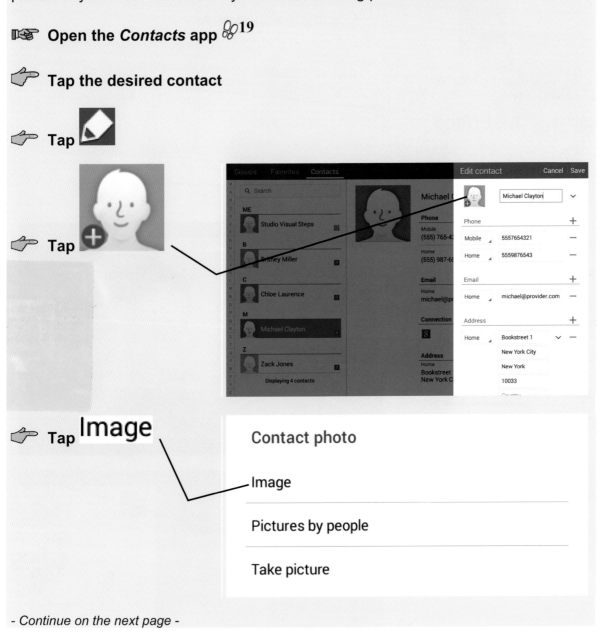

☞ **Tap Image**

Contact photo

Image

Pictures by people

Take picture

- Continue on the next page -

Select the photo album that contains the photo:

☞ **Tap the desired album**

☞ **Tap the desired photo**

☞ **Tap** Crop picture

☞ **Tap** Just once

If you wish, you can use the blue handles to change the position of the blue frame:

The part of the photo that lies within the frame is the part that will be used.

☞ **Tap** Done

The photo has been added to the contact data:

☞ **Tap** Save

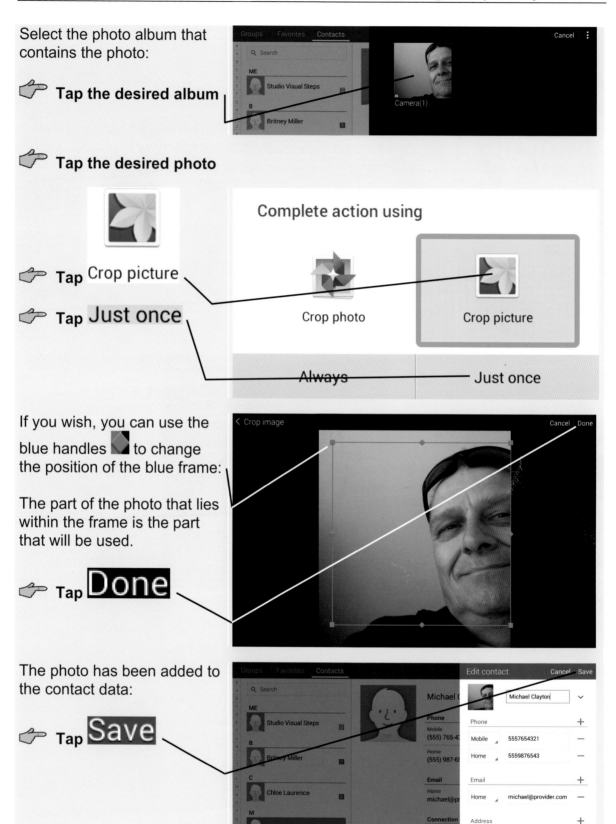

Tip

Add or delete a field
This is what you do if you want to add an extra field:

☞ **Tap the desired contact**

☞ **Tap**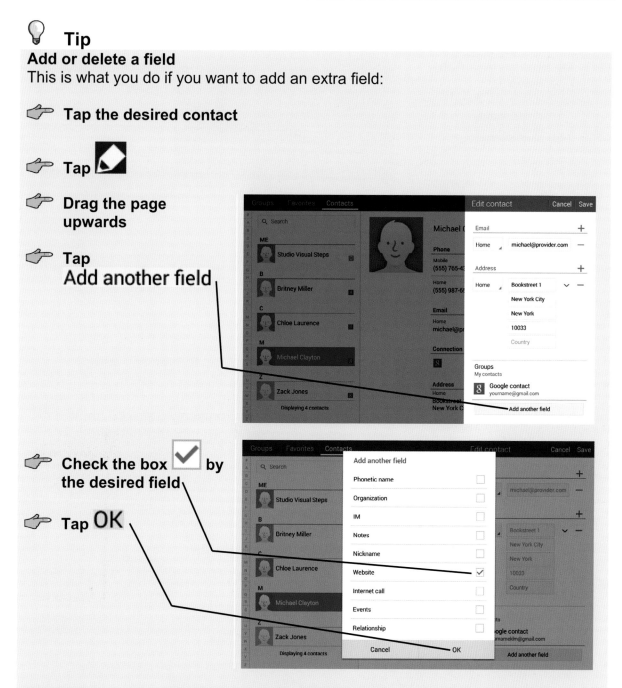

☞ **Drag the page upwards**

☞ **Tap**
Add another field

☞ **Check the box** ✓ **by the desired field**

☞ **Tap OK**

The field has been added to the contact data. Now you can continue editing the contact data and save your changes, as you did before.

- Continue on the next page -

This is how you delete the field:

☞ **By the desired field, tap** ▬

☞ **Tap** Save

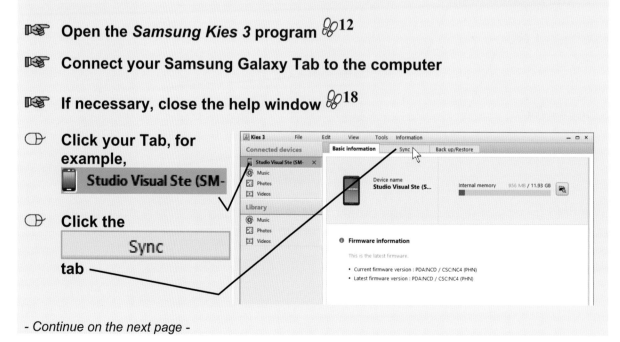

💡 **Tip**

Synchronize contacts
The contacts you have saved in your *Google* account will automatically be synchronized with all the devices on which you use this *Google* account. If you already use a different program on your computer for managing your contacts, you may be able to synchronize the contact data with your Samsung Galaxy Tab. It is possible, for example, to synchronize with *Microsoft Office Outlook* contacts.

On your computer:

☞ **Open the *Samsung Kies 3* program** 👣12

☞ **Connect your Samsung Galaxy Tab to the computer**

☞ **If necessary, close the help window** 👣18

⊕ **Click your Tab, for example,** 📱 **Studio Visual Ste (SM-**

⊕ **Click the** Sync **tab**

- Continue on the next page -

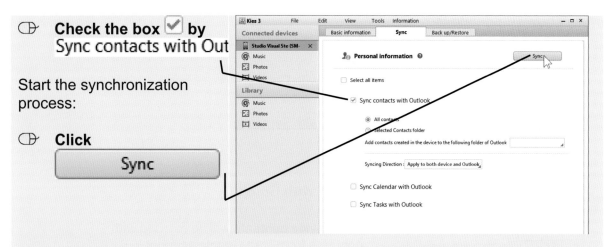

⊕ **Check the box** ☑ **by**
Sync contacts with Out

Start the synchronization
process:

⊕ **Click**

> Sync

The contacts will be synchronized. You will see the progress in the bottom right-hand corner of your screen.

Now the contacts have also been copied to the *Contacts* app on your Samsung Galaxy Tab. Because you have saved the contacts you added on your tablet in your *Google* account, these contacts have not been saved in the *Windows Contacts* and in the *Samsung Kies 3 Library* on your computer. But this is not necessary, since you have saved these contacts online, so you can access them on different devices.

☞ **Safely disconnect the Samsung Galaxy Tab from the computer** 𝄞[13]

☞ **Close** *Samsung Kies 3* 𝄞[7]

☞ **Open the** *Contacts* **app** 𝄞[19]

The new contacts have been
added. They have not been
saved in your *Google*
account. If you want you can
merge these accounts:

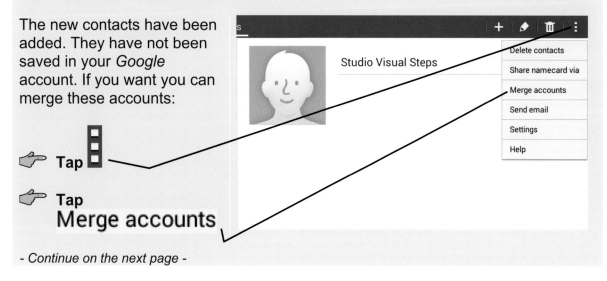

☞ **Tap** ⁝

☞ **Tap**
Merge accounts

- Continue on the next page -

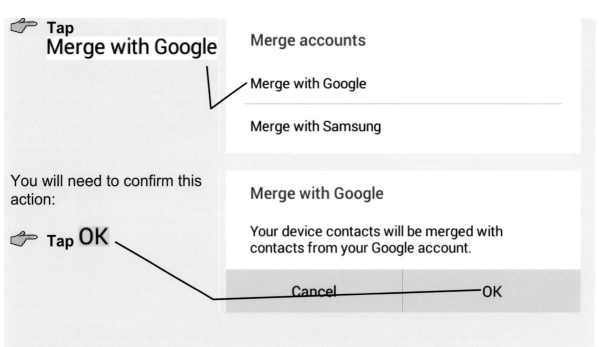

☞ **Tap**
Merge with Google

You will need to confirm this action:

☞ **Tap OK**

Now all contacts have been saved in your *Google* account as well.

💡 **Tip**

Synchronize your calendar with Outlook
If you keep your calendar on your computer in *Outlook*, you can synchronize this calendar with your Tab. Then the calendar events from *Outlook* will be added to *My Calendar* in the *S Planner* app, and not to the *Google* calendar you have used in this chapter. But you will still be able to simultaneously view the items in the *S Planner* app. The events from your *Google* calendar will not be added to your *Outlook* calendar.

☞ **Open the *Samsung Kies 3* program** ✇12

☞ **Connect your Tab to the computer**

☞ **If necessary, close the help window** ✇18

⊕ **Click your Tab, for example** 📱 **Studio Visual Ste (SM-**

⊕ **Click the** Sync **tab**

- Continue on the next page -

☞ **Check the box** ☑ **by** Sync Calendar with

By default, all the events will be synchronized:

If you do want to synchronize a specific folder with events, you need to click the radio button ⦿ by Selected Schedule f

and check the box ☑ with the desired option(s):

☞ **Check if the other options are not selected with checkmarks** ☑, **such as the** Sync Tasks with Outlook **option**

If this is the case:

☞ **Uncheck the boxes** ☑

Start the synchronization process:

☞ **Click** Sync

The events from the *Outlook* calendar will be transferred to the *My Calendar* diary in the *S Planner* app:

☞ **Safely disconnect the Tab from the computer** 👣[13]

☞ **Close** *Samsung Kies 3* 👣[7]

On the Tab:

☞ **Open the** *S Planner* **app** 👣[20]

Now the *Outlook* events will also be visible in the *S Planner* app.

💡 Tip

Conduct a video conversation with Hangouts
With the *Hangouts* app you can use the Samsung Galaxy Tab to make video calls. In order to use *Hangouts* you need to have an Internet connection and a *Google* account. If you do not yet have a *Google* account, you can read how to create one in *Chapter 1 section 1.12 Creating and Adding a Google Account*. You contacts will also need to have a *Google* account and use *Hangouts*.

First, you open the app:

On the Tab 4:

 **Tap**

On the TabPro and NotePro:

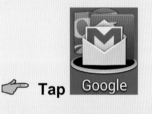 **Tap** Google

☞ **If necessary, drag the screen from right to left**

 **Tap** Hangouts

- Continue on the next page -

Invite a contact to become your friend in *Hangouts*:

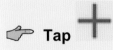 **Tap**

If you want to send an invitation you will need to have your contact's email address:

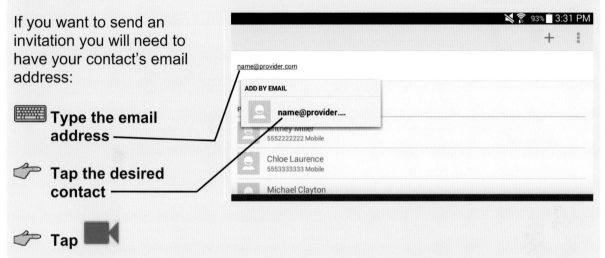

Type the email address

Tap the desired contact

Tap

The program will try to establish a connection. You will hear the phone ring and you will see the image of your own camera.

If your contact accepts the video chat, you will see and hear your contact:

You can use the button you can mute the sound of your microphone:

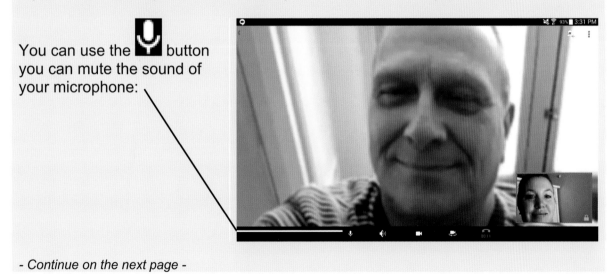

- Continue on the next page -

If you want to end the call:

 **Tap**

Use the ⬛ button to switch to the camera on the rear side of the Tab. In this way you can make video calls with contacts from all over the world.

You can also make video calles with the free *Skype* app. With this app you can call other *Skype* users. You can download this app in the *Play Store*. In *Chapter 6 Downloading Apps* you will read more about downloading apps.

5. Maps, Google Search, and Managing Files

In the *Maps* app you can look up addresses and well-known locations. You can view these locations on a regular map and on a satellite photo as well. Many locations allow you to use the *Google Street View* function. This makes it look as if you are actually there, on the spot. Once you have found the desired location, you can get directions on how to get there.

Google Search is the search function on your Samsung Galaxy Tab. This function enables you to search all the apps, contacts, messages, and music stored on your Samsung Galaxy Tab. If you are connected to the Internet you can also use this function to search the Internet.
Furthermore, you can also manage files on your tablet. For example, files or photos you have downloaded from the Internet. You can find these files with the *Downloads* app or the *My Files* app. You can place these files in a specific folder, or delete them, among other things.
In this chapter, you will learn more about these useful apps. You will also learn how to close an app or turn it off.

In this chapter you will learn how to:

- determine your present location in the *Maps* app;
- view a satellite photo;
- find and view a location with *Street View*;
- get directions;
- search with the *Google Search* app;
- work with the *My Files* app;
- close apps.

Please note:

While you are using your Tab, you may see some screens that provide additional information about the operation of an app or the keyboard. You can read the information and tap **Done** or OK afterwards.

5.1 Maps

You can use the *Maps* app to find a location and get directions for a future journey. You do need to have an Internet connection established in order to use this function. This is how you open the *Maps* app:

☞ Unlock or turn on the Samsung Galaxy Tab 🐾**9**

☞ If necessary, tap

☞ If necessary, tap Apps

☞ Tap Maps

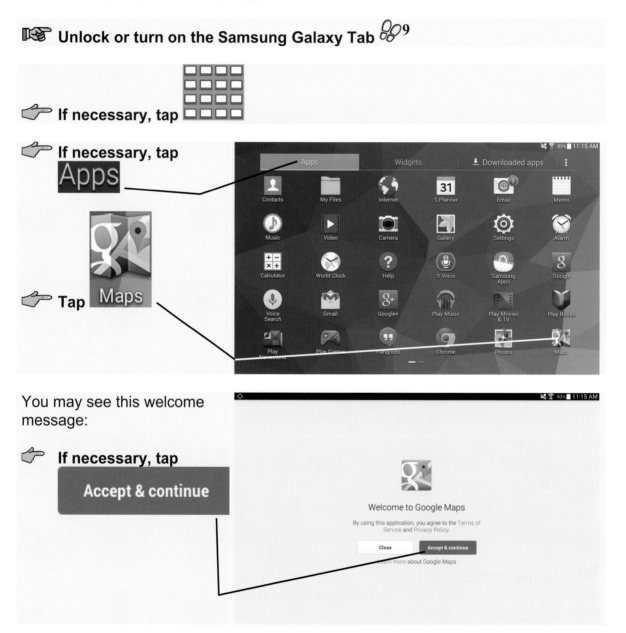

You may see this welcome message:

☞ If necessary, tap Accept & continue

In the next screen you will be asked whether or not you would like to allow *Google* to use your location information. In the example this option is chosen:

☞ **If necessary, tap**

Yes, I'm in

You will see a map of your country:

Of course, you will see a different location from the one used in this example.

You can change the view of the map by adding layers:

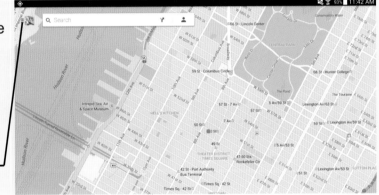

☞ **Tap**

🖐 **Please note:**

You may see a screen regarding tips for improving the accuracy of your location. To improve the accuracy:

☞ **Tap Settings**

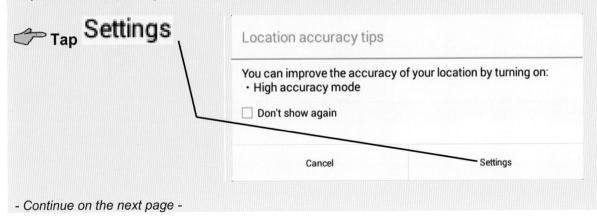

- Continue on the next page -

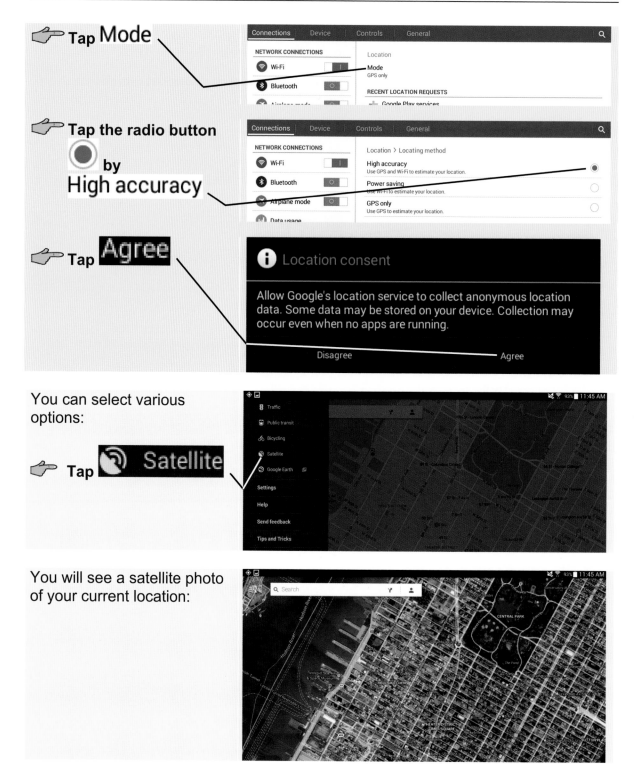

☞ Tap Mode

☞ Tap the radio button ⬤ by High accuracy

☞ Tap Agree

You can select various options:

☞ Tap 🛰 Satellite

You will see a satellite photo of your current location:

5.2 Searching for a Location with Street View

There are times when you want to find a certain location. If you have an address available you can search for it directly in *Maps.* You can also look for well-known public places or a city's local attractions:

☞ **Tap** 🔍 Search
(Search)

⌨ **Type:** Guggenheim
Museum

☞ **Tap** 🔍

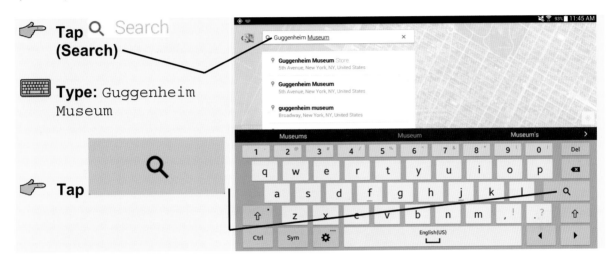

The location is represented by an icon: .

Zoom in on the location:

☞ **Spread two fingers
across the map**

💡 **Tip**

Zoom out
Move two fingers towards one another (pinch) in order to zoom out.

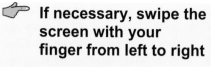 **If necessary, swipe the screen with your finger from left to right**

This is what you see on the screen, more or less:

Once you have found a location in *Maps*, you can look at it more closely using the *Street View* function:

Tap
Solomon R. Guggenheim M

Tap the photo containing the Street View text

The location will be opened in *Google Street View*:

You will find yourself in front of the museum. In order to view the top of the museum:

☞ **Drag the screen from top to bottom**

You will see the image moving upwards:

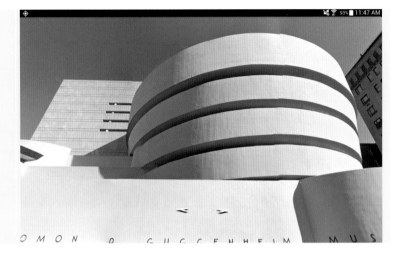

You can also take a look at the surroundings:

☞ **Drag the screen from bottom to top**

☞ **Drag the screen from right to left**

You will be looking down the street:

By using the 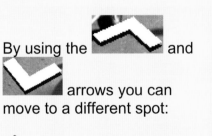 and

arrows you can move to a different spot:

☞ **Tap the top arrow**

three times

You will proceed further down the street:

If you want to go back to the map view:

☞ **Press the Back key**

↫

5.3 Getting Directions

Once you have found the desired location, you can get directions to it, like this:

☞ Tap

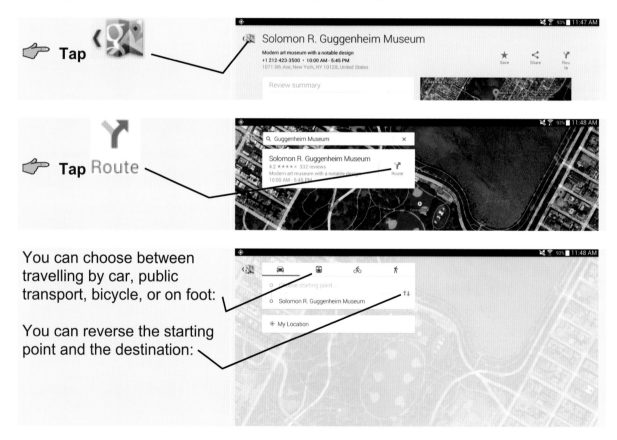

☞ Tap Route

You can choose between travelling by car, public transport, bicycle, or on foot:

You can reverse the starting point and the destination:

Enter a new starting point:

By
Choose starting point...,
type: `Empire Hotel`

Tap

Right away, the program will compute driving directions for a trip from the Empire Hotel to the Guggenheim Museum. The blue line indicates the route: ———

Here you see the number of miles and the estimated travel time, based on the current traffic conditions for this trip:

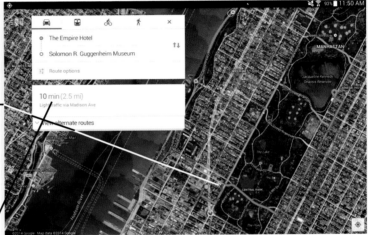

In order to display the instructions:

Tap
10 min (2.5 mi)

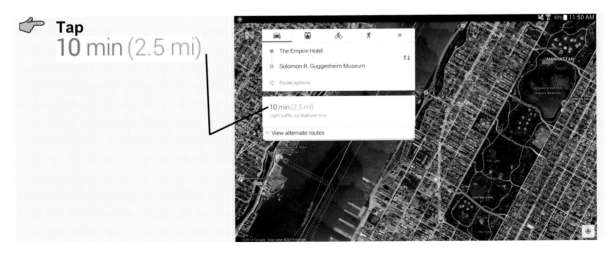

You will see the instructions:

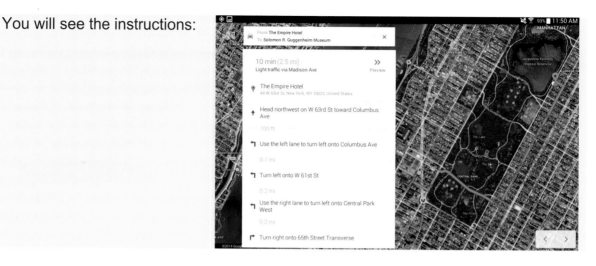

By tapping the instructions you can display parts of the route:

 **Tap** ↰ Use the right lane to turn left onto Central Park West

You will see part of the route:

You can follow the route step by step, by constantly tapping the next instruction. For now this will not be necessary.

If necessary:

👉 **Swipe downwards over the instructions**

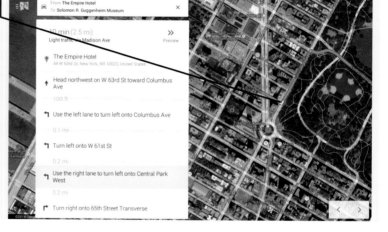

This is another way of viewing the route:

»

👉 **Tap** Preview

Now you see the route from a different viewpoint.

By tapping the grey bar at the top on the left or right-hand side, you can view the next or previous instruction.

By zooming out you can display the entire route:

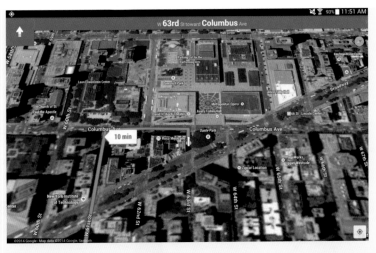

☞ **Move two fingers towards each other, across the map**

☞ **Repeat this gesture until you see the entire route**

You will see the whole route:

Now you can return to the satellite view and delete these directions. To do that:

☞ **Press the Back key**

☞ **Tap** ✕

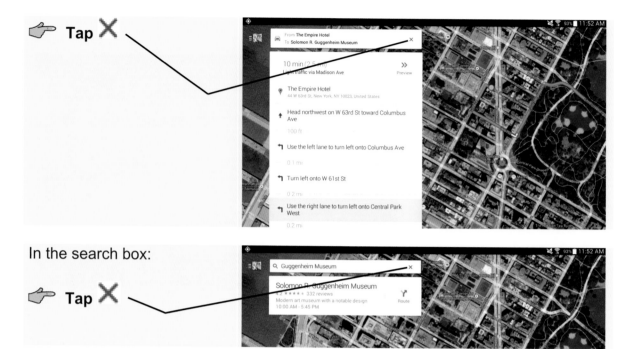

In the search box:

☞ **Tap** ✕

The directions will be deleted. You can return to your current location, like this:

In the bottom right-hand corner of the screen:

☞ **Tap**

You will see your current location again.

▨☞ **Go back to the home screen** 🐾³

5.4 Searching

Google Search is the app that provides search functionality for your Samsung Galaxy Tab. Here is how you open *Google Search*:

☞ **Tap** [Google]

First, you will see some information about *Google Now*:

☞ **Tap** [NEXT]

You will see one more screen regarding the activation of *Google Now*. In the bottom left-hand corner of the screen:

☞ **Tap** No, maybe later.

If Wi-Fi and the mobile data network (if applicable) have been turned off, the *Google Search* app will search the content of your tablet only. If an Internet connection has been enabled, the Internet will be searched as well.

In this example we are going to see which items are found beginning with the letter m:

Type: m

You will see the Internet search suggestions for words that begin with the letter m:

Below there are various apps that begin with an m:

☞ **Go back to the home screen** ℒℴ³

♀ **Tip**

Open *Google Search* from the apps list
You can also open the *Google Search* app using the apps list:

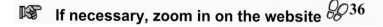

☞ **Tap** ⬚⬚⬚ , Google **(on de TabPro and NotePro),** Google

5.5 The My Files App

When you save a file, from a website for example, the file will be saved automatically to your tablet. You can find these files in the *My Files* app. You can see how this works by saving the table of contents (PDF file) from this book:

☞ **Open the *Internet* app** ℒℴ³⁴

☞ **Open the www.visualsteps.com/samsungtab4 web page** ℒℴ³⁵

You will see the website that goes with this book. This is how you download the table of contents:

☞ **If necessary, zoom in on the website** ℒℴ³⁶

Tap
Table of contents

A part of the window may now be enlarged:

Tap
Table of contents

Now the download process will begin. This is indicated by the ⬇ icon at the top of your screen.

You can find the file in the *Notification Panel*.

☞ **Go back to the home screen** 🦶³

☞ **Open the *Notification Panel*** 🦶¹

Here you can see the downloaded files. To open the file:

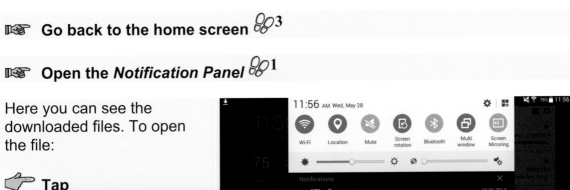

Tap

675.pdf
Download complete.

The file will be opened:

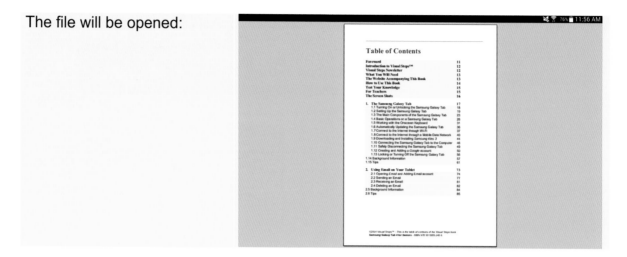

You can also find other files using the *My Files* app, for instance, downloaded files such as photos and videos that have been saved to your tablet. You can search for the file you just downloaded with this app.

☞ **Go back to the home screen** ℘³

☞ **Tap** 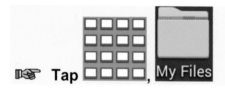, **My Files**

You will see different categories. The downloaded file has been saved in the *Device storage* section:

☞ **Tap**

📄 **Documents**

Please note:

If you have a memory card inserted in your Tab, the file may have been stored in the 🗄 **SD card** folder. In that case you need to tap 🗄 **SD card**.

You will see the PDF file that has been saved:

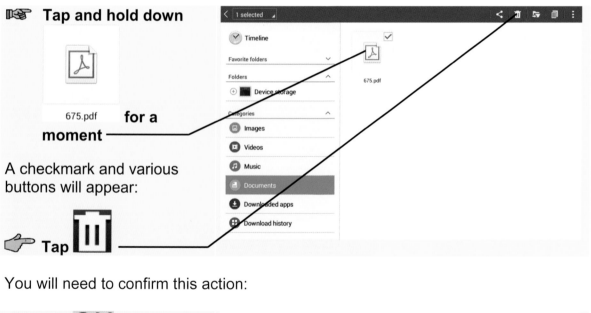

If you tap a file name, the file will be opened. For now this will not be necessary.

You can use this same method to find all sorts of files on your Tab. For example, any pictures you take in the exercises for *Chapter 7 Photos and Video* can be found in the *Images* folder. You can read more about transferring photos to your Tab from a memory card in the *Tip Transferring Photos from Memory Card to Tab* at the end of *Chapter 7 Photos and Video*.

If you want to delete the downloaded file:

☞ **Tap and hold down**

675.pdf **for a moment**

A checkmark and various buttons will appear:

☞ **Tap** 🗑

You will need to confirm this action:

☞ **Tap OK**

Delete

1 item will be deleted.

Cancel   OK

You can return to the home screen of the app like this:

☞ **Press the Back key**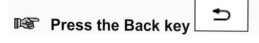

☞ **Go back to the home screen** ൬൬³

5.6 Closing Apps

By now you have used various apps on your Samsung Galaxy Tab. After you have worked with an app, you have always gone back to the home screen. When you do this, some of the apps are not actually closed and will stay active in the background. This is usually not a problem, because the Samsung Galaxy Tab uses hardly any energy (or no energy at all) when it is locked. It also makes the app accessible right away, when you unlock the tablet. But if you really want to close or quit a particular app, you can do that as follows:

☞ **Press the Recent Apps key**

You will see the apps you have recently used:

☞ **Press your finger on an app, for example,**

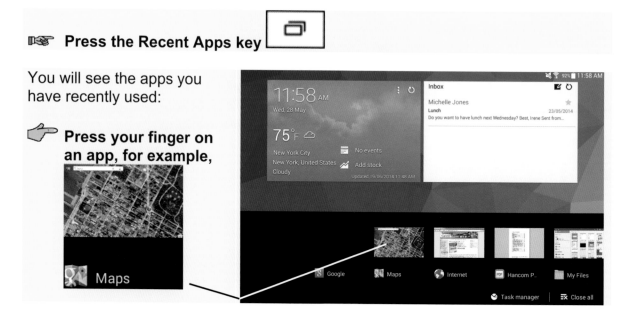

☞ **Tap**
Remove from list

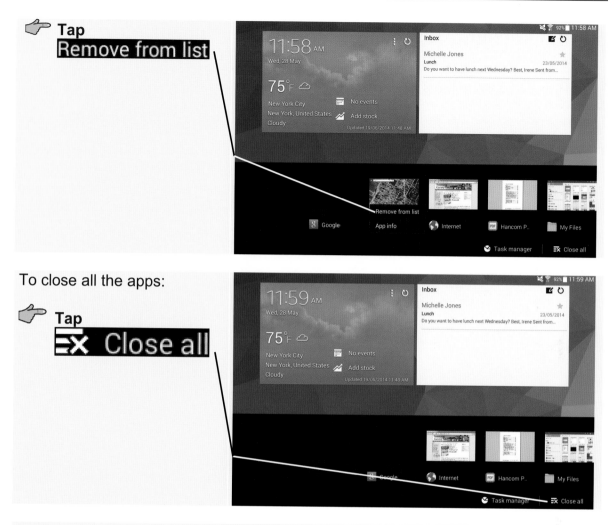

To close all the apps:

☞ **Tap**
⊒x Close all

🕮 **Lock or turn off the Samsung Galaxy Tab, if you wish** 👣**14**

In this chapter you have learned how to use the *Maps* and *My Files* apps, among other things, and you have learned how to find items on your Tab. In the *Tips* at the end of this chapter you will find a summary and brief description of the apps that have not been discussed at length in this book.

5.7 Background Information

Dictionary

Downloads	This app provides direct access to the folder that contains the files that have been downloaded to the Samsung Galaxy Tab.
Maps	An app with which you can find addresses and locations, get directions, and view satellite photos.
My Files	This app gives you access to the files stored on your Tab.
Search	Also called *Google Search*. The search function on the Samsung Galaxy Tab.
Street View	A service by *Google* that offers panoramic views on street level.

Source: User manual Samsung Galaxy Tab, Wikipedia

5.8 Tips

 Tip

Extensive information in Maps

You can find other information about many locations, such as the address or website link:

You may also see reviews posted by previous visitors:

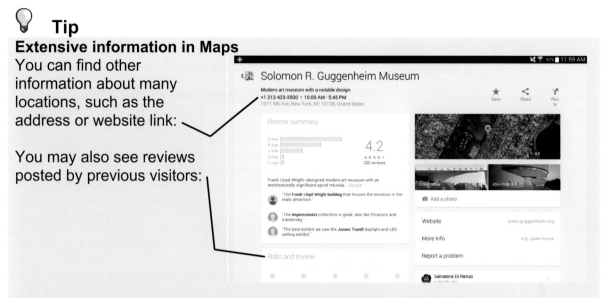

The various buttons in this screen can perform the following actions:

Use this button to save the location as a bookmark.

Use this button to share information about the location with others.

Use this button to get directions.

 Tip

Downloads

On the TabPro and NotePro, the downloaded files can also be found in the *Downloads* app:

☞ **Open the *Downloads* app** ✌️37

You will see the downloaded file:

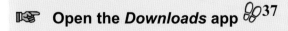

🔆 Tip

Traffic info

In the *Maps* app you can display a layer with traffic information:

👉 Tap

The speed of the traffic is indicated by a color:

Green: the traffic speed is normal.

Yellow: the traffic speed has slowed down.

Red: indicates very slow traffic.

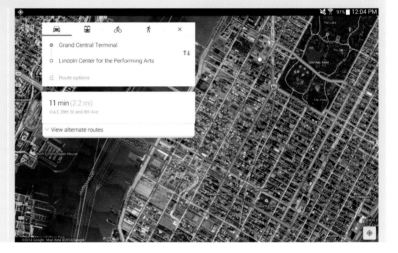

🔆 Tip

Settings for the Google Search app

You can determine which apps the *Google Search* app can search through:

👉 Tap

👉 Press the Back key ⤺

The keyboard will disappear.
In the bottom right-hand corner of the screen:

👉 Tap ⋮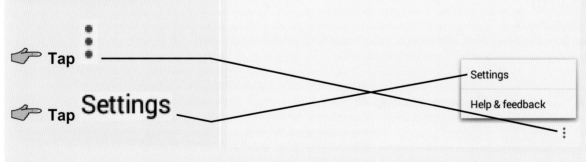

👉 Tap Settings

- Continue on the next page -

👉 **If necessary, tap**
🔍 **Tablet search**

The components that are searched by default with the *Google Search* app are marked with a . You can adjust these settings yourself:

👉 **Check the boxes ☑ to select or unselect the relevant option(s)**

👉 **Press the Back key** ⤺

💡 **Tip**

Summary of other apps

Your Samsung Galaxy Tab has many other standard apps installed that are not discussed in this book. Below you can find a brief description of these apps. The apps that are discussed in the next chapters are not listed below.

You can use this app to set an alarm for any time you want.

Calculator.

Google's Internet browser.

Google Drive is an app that allows you to create, edit, and share documents. The documents that are created, edited, or uploaded with this app can be synchronized with a computer that has *Google Drive* installed. This app is only available on the Tab 4.

- Continue on the next page -

Dropbox

You can use the *Dropbox* app to save and share photos and documents. For example, you can take a picture with your Tab, save it, and open it directly on your computer, provided you have installed *Dropbox* there as well.

e-Meeting

The *e-Meeting* app allows you to hold meetings, or take part in meetings. The app also lets you swap files with other participants. This app is only available on the TabPro.

Flipboard

Flipboard is an app that integrates news articles and information from your social media websites and displays them in a user interface that looks like a magazine. Only available on the TabPro.

Google+

A social network site by *Google*. You need to use your *Google* account for this service, and create a profile.

Google Settings

You can use this app to adjust the settings of some functions provided by *Google*.

Hancom Viewer

An Office suite that includes *Hword* (text editor), *Hcell* (spreadsheet), and *Hshow* (presentation software). With this suite you can open and edit *Microsoft Office* files, and view PDF files.

Help

This app provides help information regarding the use of the device and the apps, or the configuration of important settings.

KNOX

Knox lets you safely use your company apps on your Tab. The app separates personal and company data from each other. Only available on the TabPro.

- Continue on the next page -

Messaging

On the Samsung Galaxy Tabs with Wi-Fi and 3G/4G you can find the *Messaging* app. You can use this app to an send and receive text messages. Your mobile service provider will charge you for this service.

Phone

You can use this app to make phone calls. Only for Tabs with Wi-Fi + 3G/4G.

Photos

An app that provides access to *Google Photos*.

Play Books

Use this app to read books on your Tab.

Play Games

This app can be used to download free and paid games. You will need to have a *Samsung* account in order to use this service.

Play Newsstand

Play Newsstand gives you additional options for viewing the news items that interest you the most. You can also view news and background articles that contain audio and video.

Play Movies & TV

You can use this app to download, rent, and watch movies and TV series.

Play Music

An app that provides access to your *Google Play* music library, on every computer and on up to ten *Android* devices. All your music will be saved online, so you do not need to worry about synchronizing or storage space.

- Continue on the next page -

Remote PC

You can use this app to display your computer screen on your tablet, and operate it right from your tablet. In order to do this, you need to connect your computer and tablet through Wi-Fi or a local network. Only available on the TabPro.

S Voice

This app lets you give voice commands to your Tab, for example, to make a call to a certain phone number, send messages, take notes, or execute other tasks.

Samsung Apps

Samsung Apps is an online store owned by Samsung, where you can download both free and paid apps. In order to do this you will need to have a Samsung account.

Samsung GO

An app that keeps you posted on the latest news and current information.

SideSync 3.0

You can use this app to operate the screen of your smartphone from your tablet. Only available on the TabPro.

Video

An app with which you can rent movies, at a certain rate.

Voice Search

You can use this app to open *Google*, and give voice commands.

- Continue on the next page -

This app lets you host and attend teleconferences. The app has various other features, as well. Only available on the TabPro.

An app with which you can view the local time or other times from different locations around the world.

An app that lets you watch videos on *YouTube*.

💡 Tip

Play Books

You can use the *Play Books* app to download and read books on your Tab:

☞ **Open the *Play Books* app** ✂️**26**

👉 **If necessary, tap beside the window**

👉 **By** Ready to read?, **tap** Shop books

You can search various categories.

You can look for a book by using the search function:

👉 **Tap** 🔍

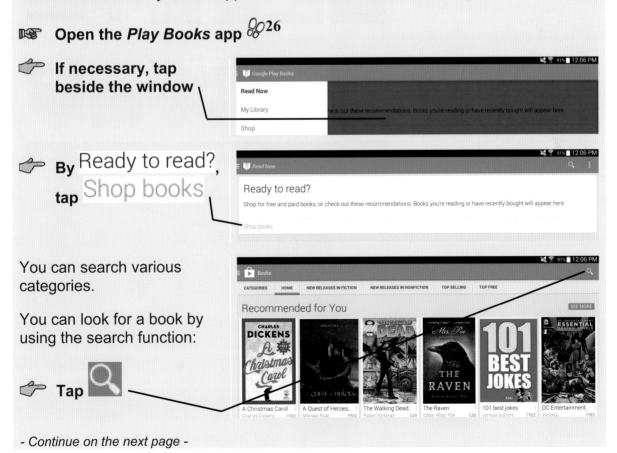

- Continue on the next page -

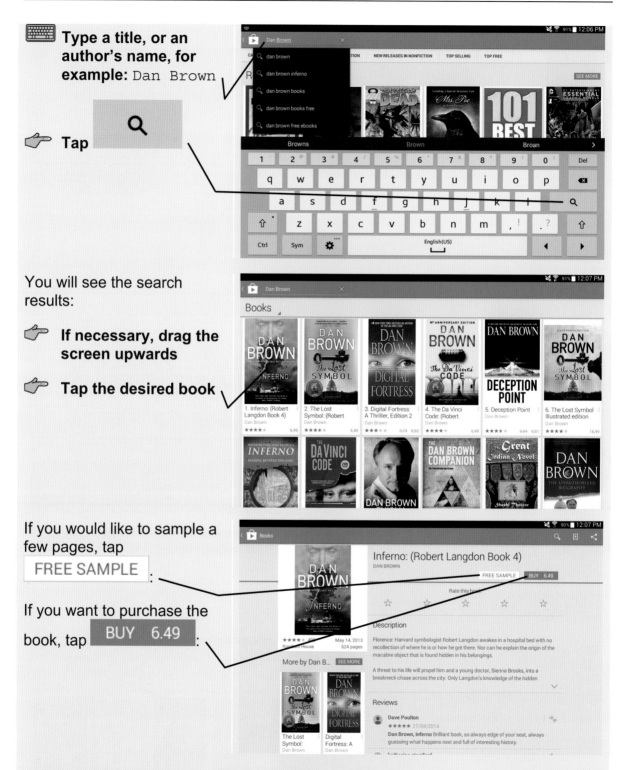

Type a title, or an author's name, for example: Dan Brown

☞ **Tap** 🔍

You will see the search results:

☞ **If necessary, drag the screen upwards**

☞ **Tap the desired book**

If you would like to sample a few pages, tap

FREE SAMPLE :

If you want to purchase the book, tap BUY 6.49 :

When you have made your selection, follow the instructions on the screen. Once the book has been downloaded, it will appear directly on your screen. By tapping the right-hand side of the screen you can go to the next page.

6. Downloading Apps

In the previous chapters you have become acquainted with a number of the standard apps that are pre-installed on the Samsung Galaxy Tab. But there are many more things you can do with this handy tablet. In the *Play Store* you will find thousands of additional apps that can be purchased or acquired for free.

There are far too many apps to list all of them in this book. There are apps for newspapers and magazines, weather forecasts, games, recipes, and sports results. You will undoubtedly find an app that interests you!

In this chapter you will learn how to download a free app from the *Play Store*. If you want to purchase an app, you can use a *Google Gift Card* to pay for it, link a credit card to your *Google* account or pay through you PayPal account. It only takes a few steps to do this.

Once you have purchased some apps, you can change the order in which they are arranged on the screen of your Tab. You can even create folders for your apps and store related apps in them. You can also delete the apps you no longer want to use.

In this chapter you will learn how to:

- download and install a free app;
- redeem a *Google Gift Card*;
- purchase and install an app;
- move apps;
- save apps in a folder;
- delete apps.

➥ Please note:

In order to buy and download apps in the *Play Store*, you need to have connected a *Google* account to your tablet. If you do not yet have a *Google* account, you can read how to create one in *section 1.12 Creating and Adding a Google Account*.

➥ Please note:

While you are using your Tab, you may see some screens that provide additional information about the operation of an app or the keyboard. You can read the information and tap **Done** or **OK** afterwards.

6.1 Downloading a Free App

In the *Play Store* you will find thousands of free apps. This how you open the *Play Store*:

☞ **Unlock or turn on the Samsung Galaxy Tab** 🦶⁹

☞ **Tap** Play Store

The *Play Store* is opened:

☞ **Tap** APPS

Recommended for You

You will see the **HOME** page, where a number of popular apps are highlighted. To see more apps:

☞ **Drag the screen with your finger from left to right**

You will see a list of categories with all the available apps:

☞ **Drag the list upwards**

☞ **Tap** Weather

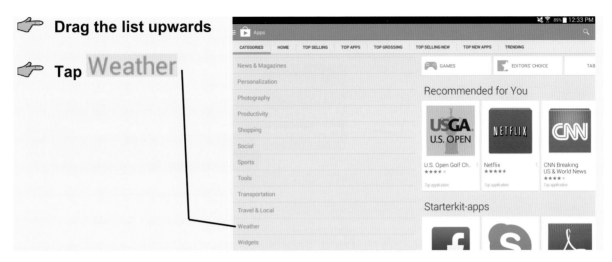

You will see a long list of popular apps that can be purchased. To view the most popular free apps in this same category:

☞ **Tap** **TOP APPS**

You will see all sorts of free apps regarding the weather. Take a look at a popular free app:

☞ **If necessary, drag the screen upwards**

☞ **Tap** Channel

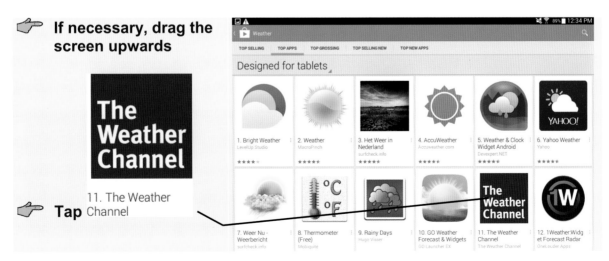

A screen will be opened with additional information about this app. If you want to download the app:

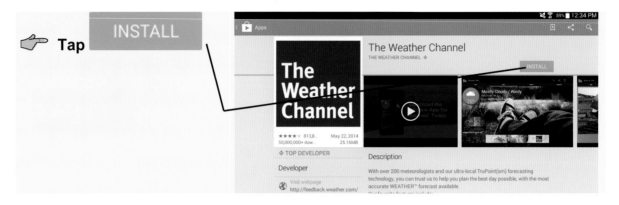

☞ **Tap** INSTALL

You will see a list of permissions required, in order for the app to function properly on your tablet. You will need to accept these permissions:

☞ **Tap**

ACCEPT

The app will be installed. After the app has been installed, you can open it:

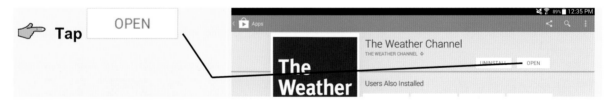

☞ **Tap** OPEN

When you open *The Weather Channel* app for the first time, you will see some additional windows first:

Agree to the terms:

☞ **Tap** Yes, I agree

You will see a screen regarding the use of your current location:

☞ Tap **Enable**

You may see an advertisement as well:

☞ Tap ✖

☞ **If necessary, tap the screen**

You will see the *The Weather Channel* app. This app will keep you posted on the current weather conditions:

 Go back to the home screen 👣³

💡 **Tip**

Update apps
In the *Tips* at the end of this chapter you can read how to update an app. From time to time, an update may be offered containing bug fixes or additional functionality.

💡 **Tip**

Managing apps
The new app will be placed on the first free spot in the apps list. If the page is full, a new page will be created. In *section 6.3 Managing apps* you can read how to move apps around on a page and between pages.

In the next section you will learn how to purchase an app.

6.2 Downloading a Purchased App

If you want to acquire an app that must be purchased first, you can pay for it with *Google Gift Card* credit, a debit or a credit card, or a PayPal account. When you try to download an app that is not free, you will be asked which one of these payment methods you want to use.

✖ HELP! I do not have a Google Gift Card, credit card, or a PayPal account.

You can purchase a *Google Gift Card* and redeem it in the *Play Store*. You can read more about gift cards on http://play.google.com/intl/en-US_us/about/giftcards/.
The *Play Store* also accepts payment by credit card. If you do not have a credit card, you could consider getting a prepaid Visa card, MasterCard, or American Express credit card. When you have done this, you can 'charge' this card with any amount you wish. With a prepaid credit card you can purchase any item as long as it does not exceed the pre-deposited amount on the credit card. Because of this, the risk of making online payments is quite small.
Another payment method is called PayPal. PayPal acts as an intermediary, so your bank account information will not be disclosed when you pay for an item in the *Play Store*. You can pay through PayPal and choose whether to pay with your regular bank account, a debit or a credit card, or with your PayPal credit. More information can be found on the PayPal website: www.paypal.com.

➴ Please note:

In this example a *Google Gift Card* is used. If you do not have such a card, you can use a debit card, a credit card, or your PayPal account. You can also just read through this section, or if available, you can install the free version of this app.

☞ **Open the *Play Store*** ✇²¹

You will see the page for *The Weather Channel* app again. This is how you go back to the *Play Store*:

☞ **Tap**

Previously, you have searched for an app by using the categories. But you can also search directly for the name of the app you want to download:

👉 **Tap**

In this example, we are looking for the name of a popular game. In this game, the goal is to help Swampy the alligator guide water to his broken shower:

⌨ **Type:** `my water`

👉 **Tap**

This app comes in both a free and a paid version ($1.99). For this exercise, we are selecting the paid version:

👉 **Tap**
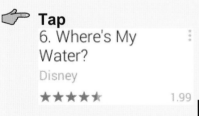
6. Where's My Water?
Disney
★★★★⯨ 1.99

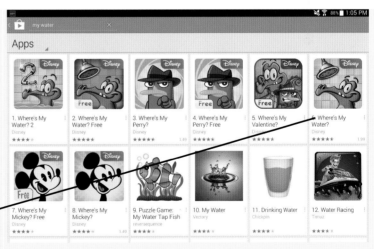

Please note: the free version offers you the opportunity to try the app before purchasing it. This version often has limited functionality and will contain advertisements.

🖐 Please note:

In the next few steps an app will be purchased. You can decide for yourself whether you want to follow the steps to buy this app. Of course, you do not need to buy the same app as shown in this example. Once you have ordered an app, you have fifteen minutes to decide whether you want to cancel the order. You can find more information about this topic in the *Tip* on page 185.

🖐 Please note:

You can only do the following steps if you have a *Google Gift Card*. If you do not have a *Google Gift Card*, you can just read through the rest of this section, or use another payment method such as a debit card, credit card, or PayPal account.

In this example, the app that is purchased costs $1.99:

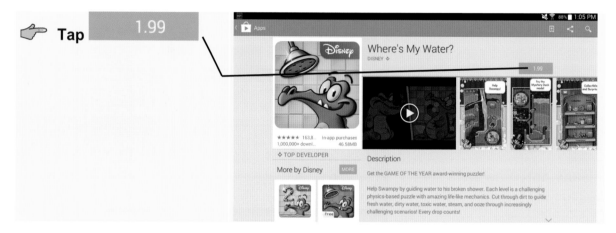

You will see the window again where the required permissions for this app are displayed:

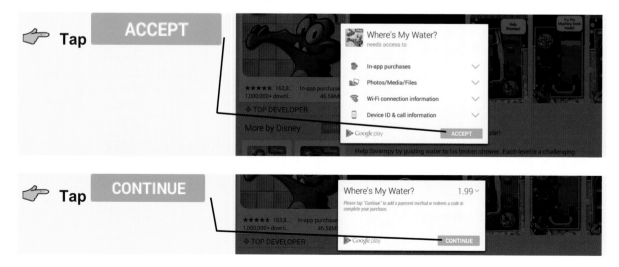

You are going to redeem the credit on your *Google Gift Card*:

☞ **Tap** 🎁 **Redeem**

Please note: if you are using a debit or a credit card, you tap 💳 **Add credit or debit card** and follow the instructions. If you want to pay with PayPal, you tap *P* **Add PayPal** and follow the instructions.

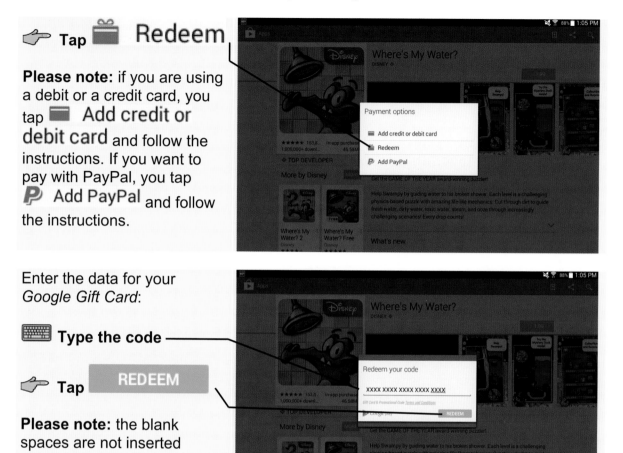

Enter the data for your *Google Gift Card*:

⌨ **Type the code** ——

☞ **Tap** **REDEEM**

Please note: the blank spaces are not inserted automatically.

The credit has been added to your *Google Play* credit. You can proceed:

☞ **Tap** 1.99

🗨 **Please note:**

If your *Google Gift Card* has already been activated, you may see fewer windows, or the windows may be displayed in a different order and not match the order described in this section. In that case, just follow the instructions in the windows that you see.

☞ **Tap**

As an extra security measure, you will be asked to enter the password for your *Google* account:

⌨ **Type the password for**
your *Google* account

☞ **Tap** CONFIRM

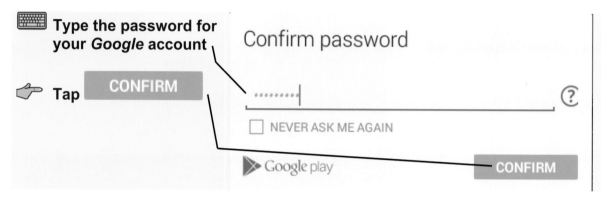

🖐 **Please note:**

It is safer not to check the NEVER ASK ME AGAIN option. If you select this option, purchases can be made in the *Play Store* and charged to your *Google Gift Card*, debit card, credit card, or PayPal account, without having to enter a password. In some games you can buy fake money in the app (while you are playing the game), and use it to bargain with. This fake money is paid for with your credit on your *Google Gift Card*, debit card, credit card, or PayPal account. If you let your children or grandchildren play such a game, for example, they will be able to purchase items without you noticing it. So it is much safer to enter the password every time you want to buy something.

You will briefly see a window with a message about the payment being successful:

☞ **Tap**

OK

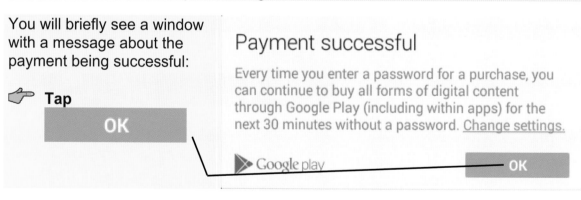

You may see a window with information about the app again:

☞ **If necessary, tap**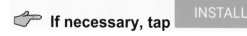

The app is downloaded and installed:

In a short while, the app will be installed. This is indicated by the OPEN button that is now displayed.

You can view the app you just downloaded a little later on. First, we will go back to the store:

Go back to the start screen of the *Play Store*:

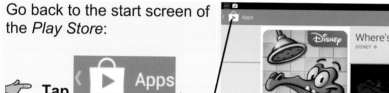

 Tap Apps

 If necessary, tap twice more

 Go back to the home screen of the Samsung Galaxy Tab 3

Tip

Cancel the purchase
You can cancel a purchase within fifteen minutes of ordering. This can be useful if you have made a mistake, or on second thought, do not like the app after all. To start the refund process:

 Tap REFUND

Please note: after fifteen minutes you will no longer see this button.

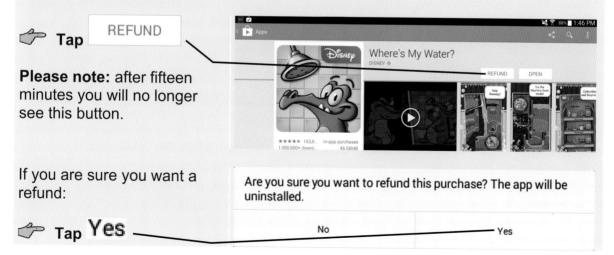

If you are sure you want a refund:

Are you sure you want to refund this purchase? The app will be uninstalled.

No	Yes

 Tap Yes

6.3 Managing Apps

You can arrange the apps on your screen in any order you wish. You do this by moving them:

For example, you will see the newly downloaded apps on the home screen:

Please note:

In order to carry out the next few steps, you need to have installed at least two apps. If you have not purchased an app, you can download another free app that interests you, as described in *section 6.1 Downloading a Free App*. Or you can use other apps to perform the steps in this section.

You can arrange the apps any way you want. This is how you move an app:

☞ **Place your finger on**

HELP! I do not see The Weather Channel app on this spot.

On your tablet, *The Weather Channel* app may not be present on this screen. In that case you can use another app to work with in this section, or leaf forward to the screen that actually contains this app.

☞ **Drag** The Weather Channel **to the**

spot where is

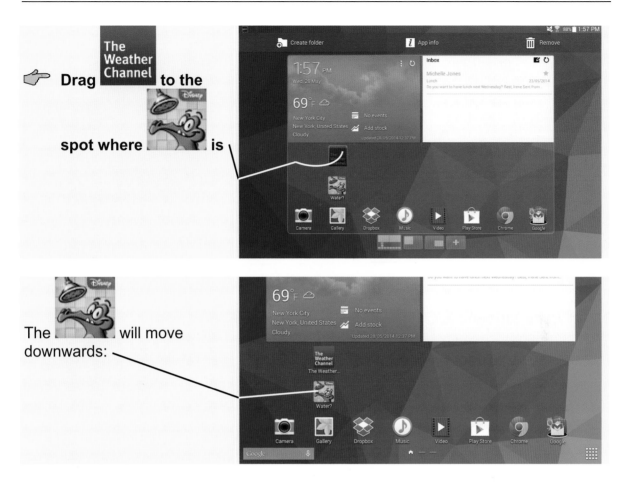

The will move downwards:

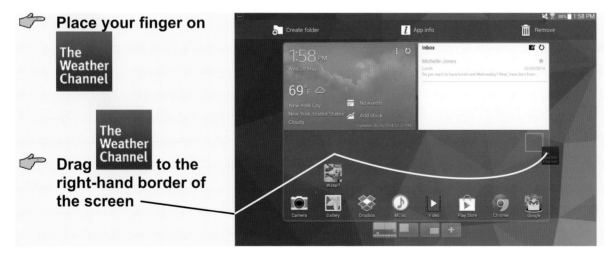

You can also move an app to another page. This is how you place an app on the second page:

☞ **Place your finger on** The Weather Channel

☞ **Drag** The Weather Channel **to the right-hand border of the screen**

When you see an other page:

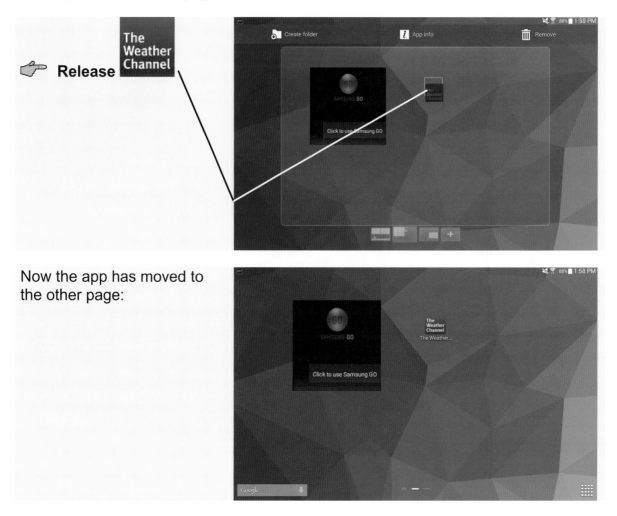

Now the app has moved to the other page:

You can also store apps together in a folder. First, move the app back to the first page:

☞ **Place *The Weather Channel* app on the first page** 🐾³⁰

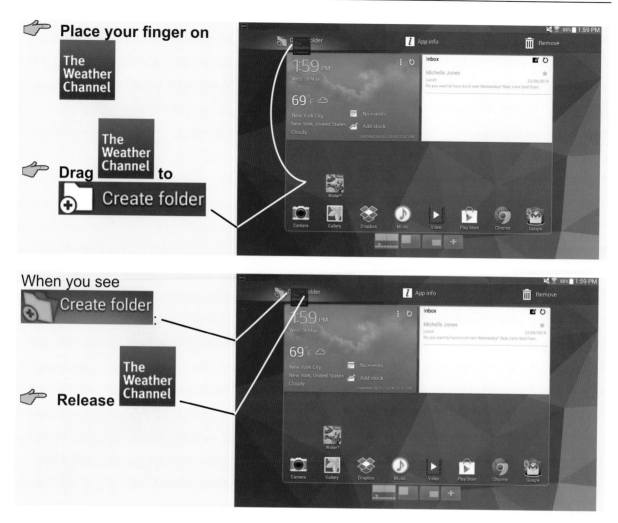

Place your finger on The Weather Channel

Drag The Weather Channel to Create folder

When you see Create folder:

Release The Weather Channel

You will see the *Create folder* window. In this example you will not be entering a name for the folder:

Tap OK

Create folder

Enter folder name.

Cancel   OK

The app has been placed in the folder:

☞ **Tap**

The folder is opened:

If you wish, you can enter a name for the folder, by **Unnamed folder**:

For now this will not be necessary.

☞ **Tap next to the folder**

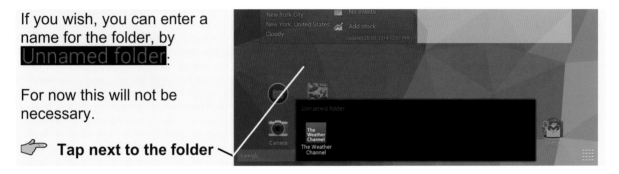

Next, you can add the other app you have downloaded to the new folder:

☞ **Drag** on top

of

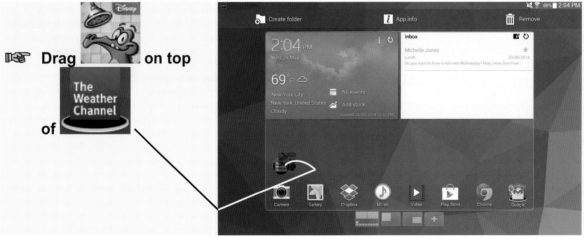

Now both apps have been included in the  folder.

This is how you view the content of the folder:

Tap

You will see both apps in the folder:

If you want, you can add some more apps to this folder.

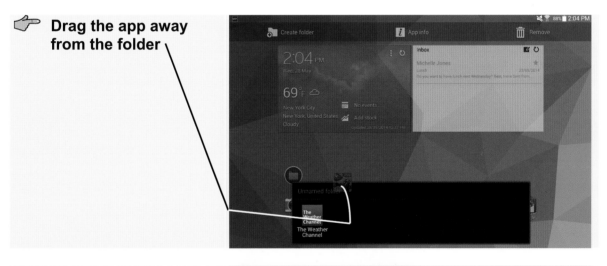

This is how you remove an app from the folder again:

Drag the app away from the folder

Now the app is on its own again, on the home screen:

You can also delete the folder. The apps that are stored in the folder will not be deleted:

☞ **Drag the folder to**

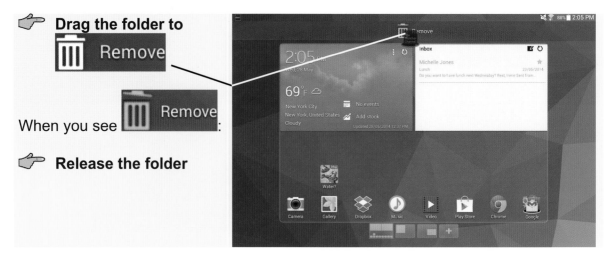

When you see 🗑 Remove :

☞ **Release the folder**

Now *The Weather Channel* app is no longer located on the home screen. On the TabPro and NotePro you can find it by tapping the ⊞ button. This will open the list showing all the apps.

6.4 Deleting an App

If you are unhappy with an app you have downloaded, you can delete it. You do this using the *Play Store*.

☞ **Tap** Play Store

☞ **Tap** ▶

☞ **Tap** My apps

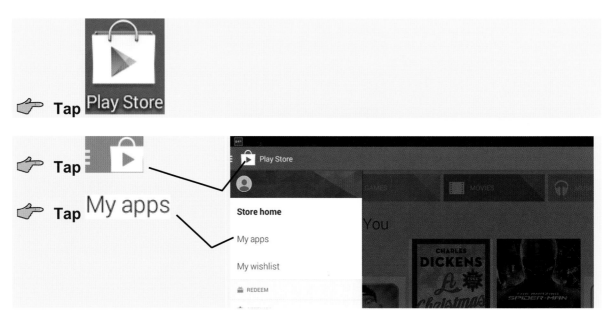

You will see the apps list. You can delete the apps you have downloaded from the *Play Store*. In this example we will delete the app called *The Weather Channel*:

If necessary, swipe the list of apps upwards

Tap the app

Tap UNINSTALL

If you really want to uninstall this app:

Tap OK

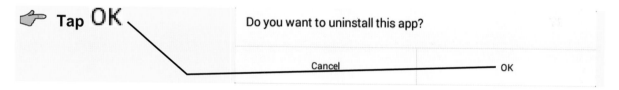

The app will be removed from the list.

Go back to the home screen ∂∂³

Lock or turn off the Samsung Galaxy Tab, if you wish ∂∂¹⁴

In this chapter you have learned how to acquire new apps by using the *Play Store*.

6.5 Background Information

Dictionary

App	Short for *application*, a program for the Samsung Galaxy Tab.
Google account	A combination of an email address and a password. You need to have a *Google* account in order to download apps from the *Play Store*.
Google Gift Card	A prepaid card with which you can purchase items from the *Play Store*.
PayPal	PayPal is a service that acts as an intermediary, so your bank account information is not displayed when you pay for something in the *Play Store*. When you pay through PayPal, you can choose whether you want to use your bank account, your debit or credit card, or your PayPal credit.
Play Store	An online store where you can download free and paid apps.
Update	Install the most recent version of the Tab's operating system, or of particular apps.

Source: User manual Samsung Galaxy Tab

6.6 Tips

💡 **Tip**

Update apps

After a while, the apps that are installed on your Tab will be updated for free. These updates may be necessary to solve certain problems (often called bug fixes). An update can also contain new functions or additional options, such as a new level in a game app. You can check for updates yourself:

☞ **Open the *Play Store*** 🦶²¹

👉 **Tap** ☰ ▶️, My apps

In this example, there is an update available for two apps:

👉 **Tap** UPDATE ALL

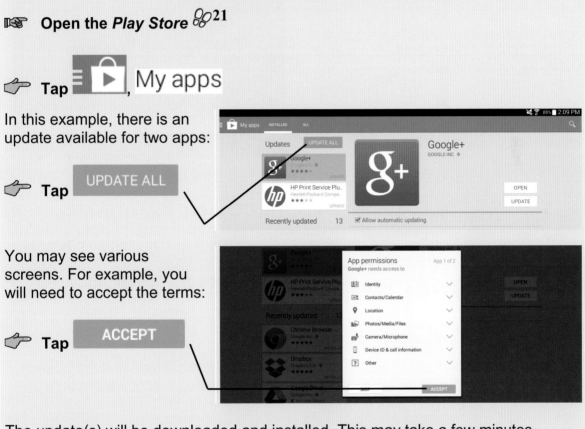

You may see various screens. For example, you will need to accept the terms:

👉 **Tap** ACCEPT

The update(s) will be downloaded and installed. This may take a few minutes.

The apps are updated.

Some apps will be updated automatically, as soon as a new update becomes available. This is indicated by the checkmark by Allow automatic updating:

- Continue on the next page -

Please note: if you are using a mobile Internet connection through 3G/4G, these automatic updates may cost you money. It is better to change these settings, so that apps are updated only when a Wi-Fi Internet connection is available.

☞ **Tap**

☞ **Tap ⚙ SETTINGS**

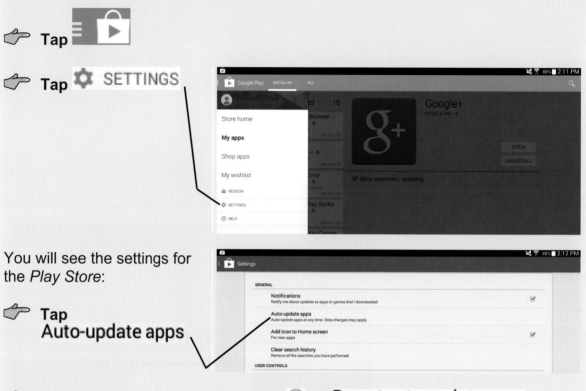

You will see the settings for the *Play Store*:

☞ **Tap**
   Auto-update apps

☞ **If necessary, tap the radio button ◉ by Do not auto-update apps**

💡 **Tip**
Download a purchased app for the second time
If you have uninstalled a purchased app, you can always download and re-install it later on, free of charge. You will need to use the same *Google* account as you did before, in order to do this.

☞ **Open the *Play Store* 👣21**

☞ **Tap , My apps**

☞ **Tap ALL**

☞ **If necessary, swipe the apps list upwards**

- Continue on the next page -

☞ **Tap**

The *Play Store* remembers that you have previously purchased the app. Instead of `1.99` you will see the `INSTALL` button.

☞ **Tap** `INSTALL`

In the next window:

☞ **Tap** `ACCEPT`

The app will be downloaded and installed. You will not be charged for this download.

💡 **Tip**

Using the Facebook app
If you use *Facebook*, you can download the *Facebook* app and use it on your Tab.

☞ **Download the *Facebook* app** 👣25

☞ **Open the *Facebook* app** 👣27

You will need to sign in with your *Facebook* account, one-time only:

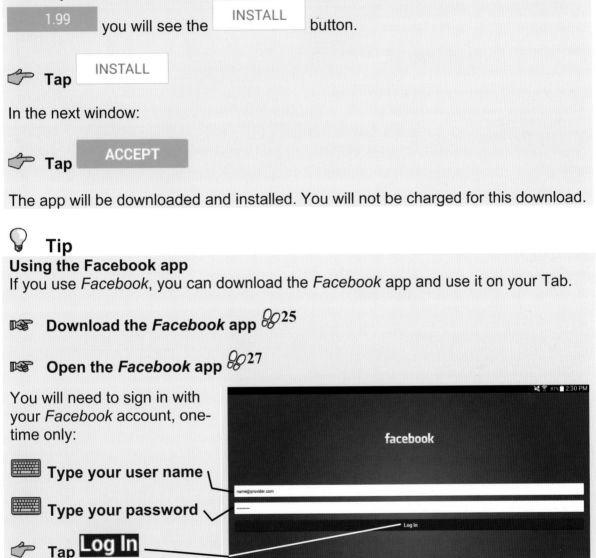

⌨ **Type your user name**

⌨ **Type your password**

☞ **Tap** `Log In`

On your News Feed page, you will see your friends' messages, and those of the celebrities or companies you follow. The messages you post on your own page, will appear in your friends' News Feed.

- Continue on the next page -

You can tap 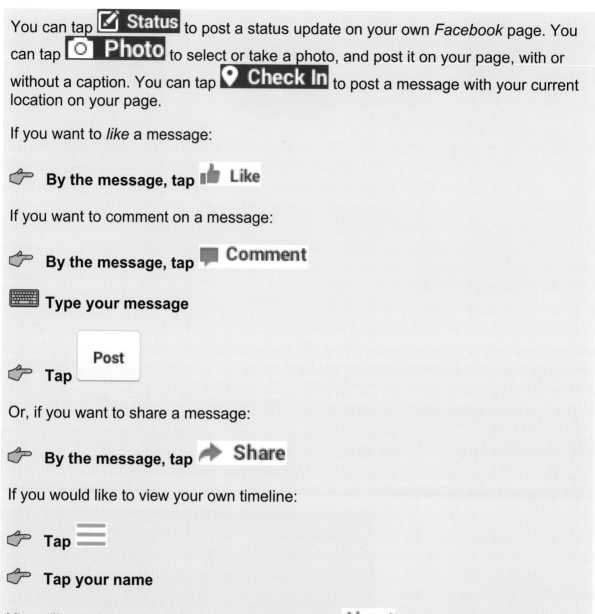 **Status** to post a status update on your own *Facebook* page. You can tap **Photo** to select or take a photo, and post it on your page, with or without a caption. You can tap **Check In** to post a message with your current location on your page.

If you want to *like* a message:

☞ **By the message, tap** **Like**

If you want to comment on a message:

☞ **By the message, tap** **Comment**

⌨ **Type your message**

☞ **Tap** **Post**

Or, if you want to share a message:

☞ **By the message, tap** **Share**

If you would like to view your own timeline:

☞ **Tap** ≡

☞ **Tap your name**

You will see the messages on your timeline. Tap **About** to go to the personal information you share on *Facebook*. Tap **Photos** to go to the photos you have uploaded to *Facebook*. Tap **Friends** to go to your list of friends. Tap **Activity Log** to display a summary of your recent activity on *Facebook*.

- Continue on the next page -

If someone reacts to your post, or comments on a message to which you have commented as well, the 🌐 button will turn into 🌐. In the same way you will see new friend requests by 👥, and new private messages by 💬.

You can use the search box to find friends or pages:

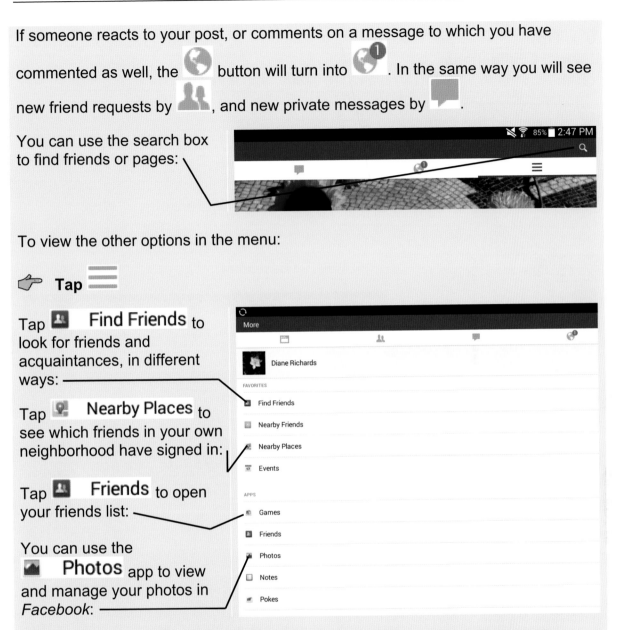

To view the other options in the menu:

👉 **Tap** ≡

Tap 🔲 **Find Friends** to look for friends and acquaintances, in different ways:

Tap 🔲 **Nearby Places** to see which friends in your own neighborhood have signed in:

Tap 🔲 **Friends** to open your friends list:

You can use the 🔲 **Photos** app to view and manage your photos in *Facebook*:

At the bottom you will find the buttons for the help options and for changing the settings. If you stay signed in, new data will be retrieved as soon as you open the *Facebook* app. If you prefer to sign off, you can do so like this:

👉 **Tap** ⏻ Log Out, **Log Out**

💡 **Tip**

Using the Twitter app

If you use *Twitter*, you can download the *Twitter* app and use it on your tablet.

☞ **Download the *Twitter* app** 𝒪𝒪²⁵

☞ **Open the *Twitter* app** 𝒪𝒪²⁸

You will need to sign in with your *Twitter* account, one-time only:

👉 **Tap** Sign In

⌨ **Type your user name**

⌨ **Type your password**

👉 **Tap** Sign In

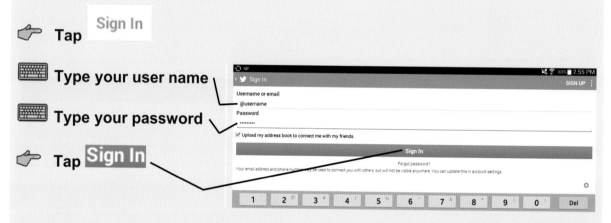

You may see a screen regarding SNS permission, in order to use your account:

👉 **Tap** Cancel

In the next two screens:

👉 **Tap** SKIP

In the next screen:

👉 **Tap** NEXT

In the next screen:

👉 **Tap** FINISH

- Continue on the next page -

Twitter wants to use your current location:

☞ **If necessary, tap** OK

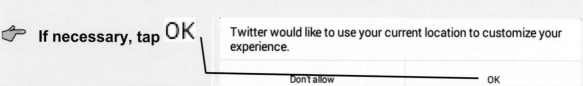

Twitter would like to use your current location to customize your experience.

Don't allow   OK

You will see your timeline, with the latest tweets of the people or companies you follow. Your own tweets will appear in the timeline of your followers.

This is how you load new tweets:

☞ **Swipe the list of messages downwards**

Use the buttons in the menu to do the following:

Tap **Home** to open the *Twitter* home page. Here you see the most recent tweets of the people or companies you follow, and your own tweets as well.

Tap **Discover** to the view a list of trends, whom to follow, and events, among other things.

Tap **Activity** to view a list of popular tweets and activities of the people you follow.

Tap ⬜ to open a list of all the comments you have received through a tweet to which you have replied. You will also see all the messages in which your user name is mentioned.

Tap ✉ to send a private message to someone you follow.

Tap 📷 to look for other *Twitter* users.

- Continue on the next page -

Tap 🔍 to look for tweets, by their subject or name.

⋮, **Visual Steps** (your name)

Tap this button to go to the page that contains your profile information. This page also contains links to the timeline with the tweets you have sent, the accounts you follow, and your own followers. This page is visible to everyone. Here you can also access your private messages. These are only visible to yourself.

This is how you send a new tweet:

☞ **In the top right-hand corner of your screen, tap** 📝

⌨ **Type your message**

☞ **Tap** TWEET

Tap 📍 to add a location to your tweet.

Tap 🖼 to take a picture and add it, or add a photo from the gallery on your Tab.

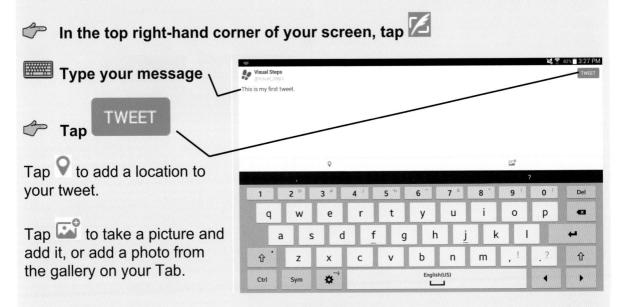

Your tweet will appear at the top of your timeline. Your followers will see your tweet appear in their timeline.

💡 **Tip**

Antivirus app

Just like on your computer, viruses can infect your Tab too. Nowadays, an antivirus app is a necessity. Although there are various antivirus apps available, most of their options are very similar. In this *Tip* the *Tablet AntiVirus Security Free* app by AVG Mobile is downloaded.

☞ **Download the *Tablet AntiVirus Security Free* app by AVG Mobile** 👣²⁵

Please note: make sure to select the version suited for a tablet. You can recognize this version by the word Tablet.

- Continue on the next page -

Activate the app:

☞ Tap

You will see the app's start screen:

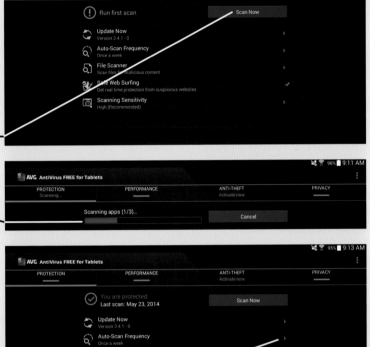

For now you do not need to change the settings, but you can allow the app to start scanning your tablet right away. To do that:

☞ Tap

During the scanning process you will see:

After the Tab has been scanned, and no viruses have been found, you can set the time interval at which the Tab will automatically scan your tablet:

☞ By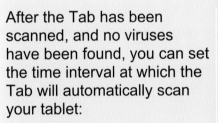

tap ◢

☞ **Tap the desired frequency**

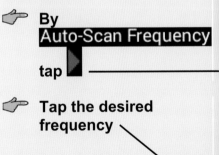

- Continue on the next page -

Other security options for your Tab are:

Update Now	With this option you can manually search for an update for the app.
File Scanner	Here you can indicate which folders to be scanned.
Safe Web Surfing	If you disable this function, you will not be protected while you are surfing the Internet. This is not recommended for regular usage.
Scanning Sensitivity	Here you can set the scan sensitivity.

Apart from the antivirus protection, this app offers a number of additional functions:

PERFORMANCE	Here you can get information about your Tab's performance. If you want more information, tap ◤ by the desired topic.
ANTI-THEFT	If you wish you can register your Tab for an anti-theft function. By registering, you will be able to block your Tab in case it is stolen, remotely lock the device and even find the current location of the Tab.
PRIVACY	Here you can secure apps with a password, or create backup copies of apps. You can temporarily try this function for fourteen days, but afterwards you will need to purchase the paid version of the app. You can also delete data on the Tab or SD (memory) card.

7. Photos and Video

The two cameras on the Samsung Galaxy Tab offer a wealth of possibilities for taking pictures and shooting videos. You can use the *Camera* app to access both of these cameras. The camera on the back of the Tab allows you to take a picture or film an interesting object. With the front camera you can create a self-portrait.

The *Gallery* app can be used to view your photos. You can view them one at a time, or display them as a slideshow on your Tab.

To play your videos you can use the *Video* app.

In this chapter you will learn how to:

- take pictures with your Samsung Galaxy Tab;
- switch between the front and rear cameras;
- film a video with your Samsung Galaxy Tab;
- view photos;
- zoom in and zoom out;
- view a slideshow;
- send a photo by email;
- print a photo;
- copy photos and videos to the computer;
- play the video you have recorded.

Please note:

While you are using your Tab, you may see some screens that provide additional information about the operation of an app or the keyboard. You can read the information and tap **Done** or **OK** afterwards.

7.1 Taking Pictures

You can use the *Camera* app to take pictures. This is how you open the app:

☞ **If necessary, unlock or turn on the Samsung Galaxy Tab** 👣**9**

☞ **If necessary, tap** ▦

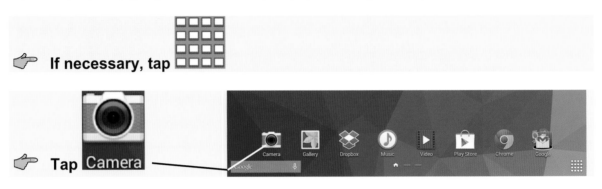

☞ **Tap** `Camera`

You will see the image that is recorded by the camera on the back of the Tab.

☞ **Point the camera towards the object you want to photograph**

🦢 **Please note:**

Make sure you have sufficient light. The Tab 4 is not equipped with a flash (the TabPro and NotePro do have a flash). If there is not enough light to take a picture, the picture will look grainy.

To take the picture:

☞ **Tap** 📷

The photo will be stored on your Tab.

💡 Tip

Zoom in and out

Spread two fingers towards or away from each other, in order to zoom in or out.

👉 **Take two more pictures** 🐾16

💡 Tip

Self-portrait

You can also choose to use the camera on the front of the Samsung Galaxy Tab. This enables you to take a picture of yourself. To switch to the front camera:

👉 **Tap**

You will see the image of the front camera:

Now you can take a picture in the same way as you did with the rear camera.

To switch back to the rear camera:

👉 **Tap**

The other main buttons on the screen of the *Camera* app are used for the functions listed below. You may need to tap the ▶ button to view more functions. Depending on the type of tablet you have, you may see additional options or not see certain options at all.

Button	Description
MODE	Set the photo mode. You can choose between the Auto, Beauty Face, Sound & Shot, Panorama, Sports and Night modes. When you select a mode you will see what this mode does.
	Set a timer for an automatic recording.

Set the exposure values.

 Adjust the camera settings.

Share photos. You can choose to share pictures with other devices using Wi-Fi Direct. You can share a photo with friends, or take a picture with the viewfinder of a connected device.

7.2 Filming

You can also use the camera to film videos:

On the Tab 4:

☞ **Drag the slider** **to**

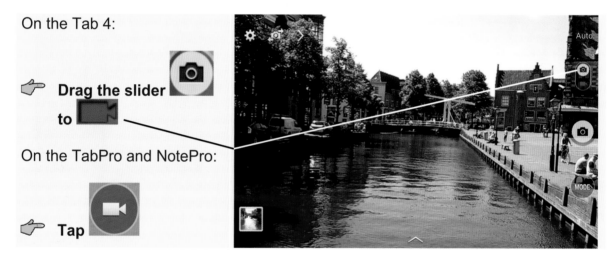

On the TabPro and NotePro:

☞ **Tap**

♡ Tip
Sideways
If you would like to play your video on a television or a larger screen, you will need to hold your Samsung Galaxy Tab in a horizontal position (landscape mode). This will provide you with a nice full-screen image.

 turns into  :

To start filming:

👉 **Tap**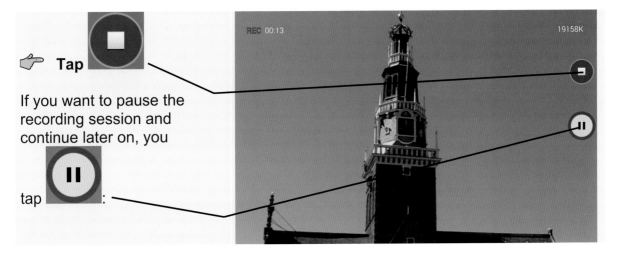

You will not see this red button on the TabPro, but the recording will start at once.

While you are recording the video, you will see a red circle ⬤ blinking at the bottom of the screen.

To stop filming:

👉 **Tap**

If you want to pause the recording session and continue later on, you

tap :

You can change the *Camera* app on the Tab 4 back to photo mode again:

👉 **Drag the slider**  **to** 📷

On the TabPro, the camera will automatically revert to photo mode.

👉 **Go back to the home screen** 👣³

7.3 Viewing Photos in the Gallery

Once you have taken a number of pictures with your Samsung Galaxy Tab, you can view them in the *Gallery* app. To open the app:

☞ **Tap** Gallery

You will see the Camera album:

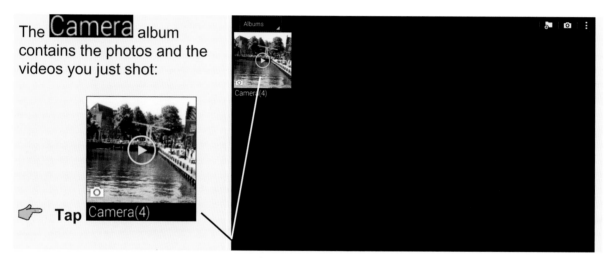

The Camera album contains the photos and the videos you just shot:

☞ **Tap** Camera(4)

You will see the pictures you have taken:

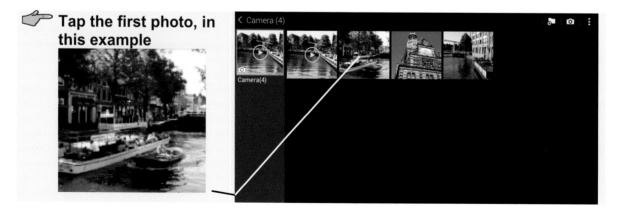

☞ **Tap the first photo, in this example**

You may see a screen regarding tags:

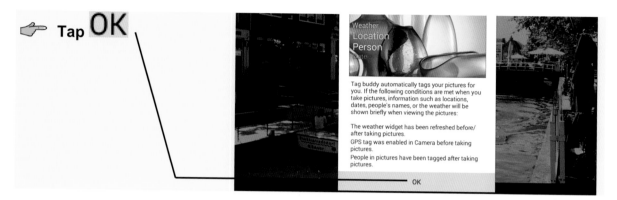

The photo will be displayed on a full screen. This is how you leaf to the next photo:

Swipe the photo from right to left

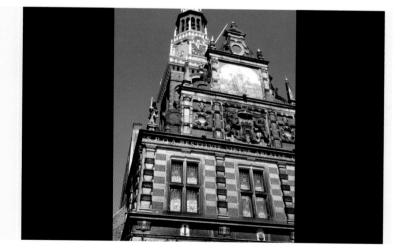

You will see the next photo. You can also zoom in on the photo. For this you can use the touch gestures you have previously used while surfing the Internet:

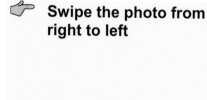

Spread your thumb and index finger across the screen

In this way, you will zoom in on the photo:

Tip

Move

You can also move the photo you have zoomed in on by dragging your finger across the screen.

To zoom out again:

Move your thumb and index finger towards each other (pinch) across the screen 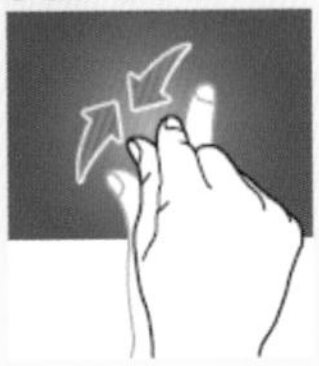

You will see the regular view of the photo again.

To go back to the first photo:

Swipe the photo from left to right

You can also view a slideshow of all the photos in an album. Here is how you do that:

If necessary, tap the photo

Tap 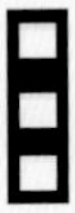

Tap Slideshow

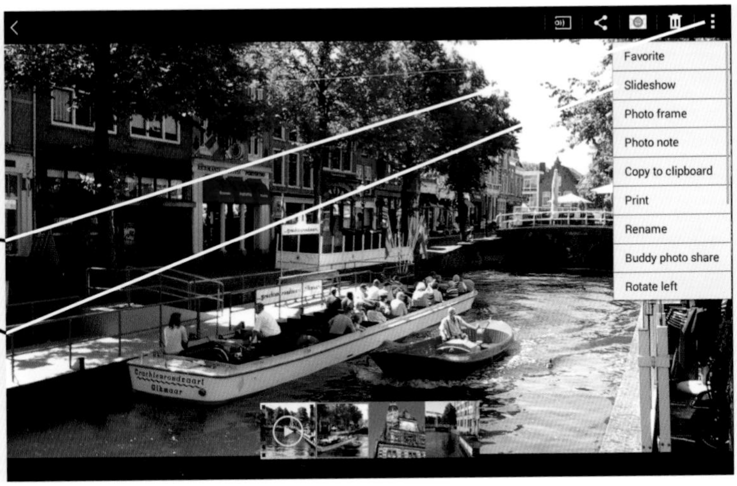

HELP! I do not see the menu bar.

The menu bar will appear when you tap the photo.

You can even add effects and music, if you wish. On the More tab you can select the speed and sorting method:

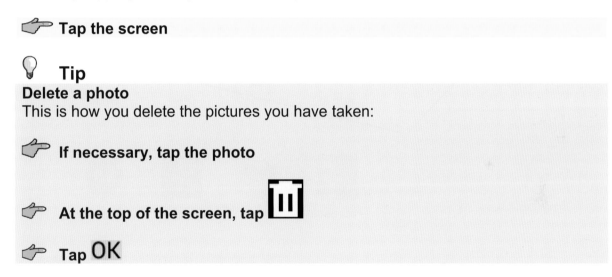

To start the slideshow:

☞ Tap **Start**

You will see the slideshow. If you have recorded a video too, this will not be displayed in the slideshow. You will only see the first frame. You can play back the video by tapping the Play button. To stop the slideshow:

☞ **Tap the screen**

💡 **Tip**
Delete a photo
This is how you delete the pictures you have taken:

☞ **If necessary, tap the photo**

☞ **At the top of the screen, tap** 🗑

☞ **Tap OK**

7.4 Sending a Photo by Email

If you have made a nice photo on your Tab, you can share it with others by email. You start by opening the photo you want to send:

☞ **Open the desired photo**

👉 **Tap the photo**

👉 **Tap**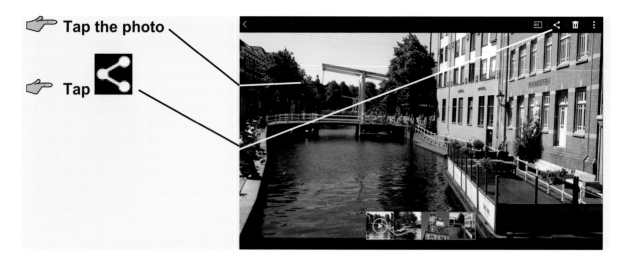

You will see a window:

On the TabPro and the NotePro:

☞ **Tap the radio button ⦿ by the desired option**

☞ **Tap** Just once

This way, you can select the size of the photo each time you want to send one.

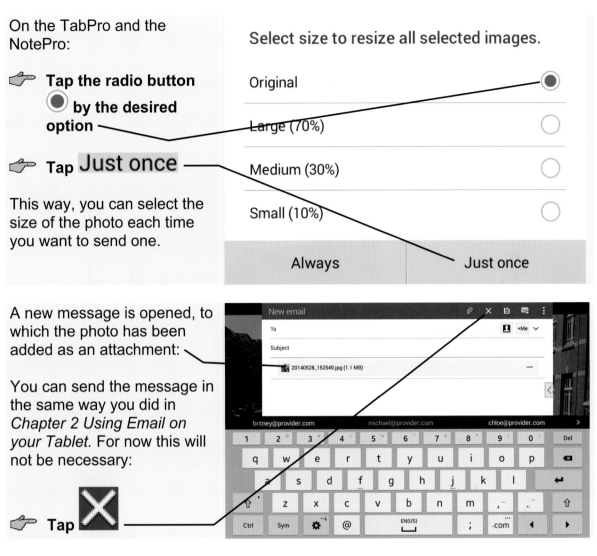

Select size to resize all selected images.

Original ⦿

Large (70%) ○

Medium (30%) ○

Small (10%) ○

Always   Just once

A new message is opened, to which the photo has been added as an attachment:

You can send the message in the same way you did in *Chapter 2 Using Email on your Tablet.* For now this will not be necessary:

☞ **Tap** ✖

You will be asked if you really want to delete the message:

☞ **Tap** Discard

Cancel email

Save this email in Drafts or discard it?

Cancel   Discard   Save

You will see the photo again.

7.5 Printing a Photo

If you have a wireless printer, you will probably be able to print through a wireless connection on your Samsung Galaxy Tab. You will need to make sure Wi-Fi is enabled. Not all printers will support this function, but if yours does, you start like this:

☞ **If necessary, turn on Wi-Fi** 👣**10**

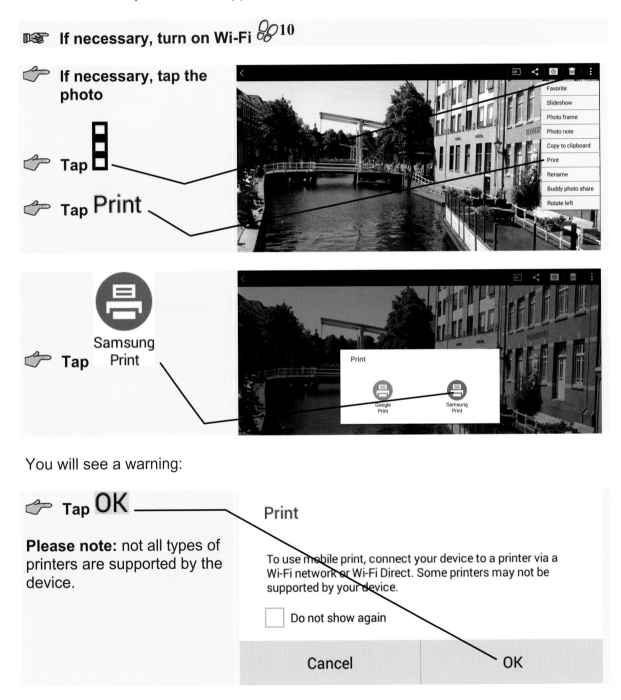

You will see a warning:

☞ **Tap OK**

Please note: not all types of printers are supported by the device.

Print

To use mobile print, connect your device to a printer via a Wi-Fi network or Wi-Fi Direct. Some printers may not be supported by your device.

☐ Do not show again

Cancel   OK

You may see a message telling you that a connection is trying to be made to the printer. If the printer has been found:

☞ **Tap the desired printer**

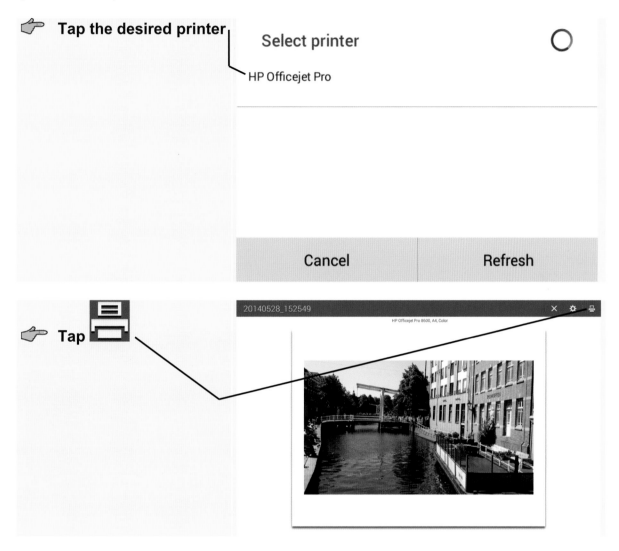

The photo will be printed.

☞ **If necessary, turn off Wi-Fi** ⏱²

☞ **Go back to the home screen** ⏱³

7.6 Copying Photos and Videos to the Computer

You can copy the photos and videos you have made with your Samsung Galaxy Tab to your computer with *Windows Explorer*. You do that like this:

☞ **Connect the Samsung Galaxy Tab to the computer**

☞ **If necessary, close the *AutoPlay* window** 8

Open *File Explorer* on the taskbar, on your desktop:

◯ **Click**

In *Windows 7* or *Vista* only:

◯ **Click** 🖥 Computer

Your Tab will be recognized by *Windows* as a portable media device:

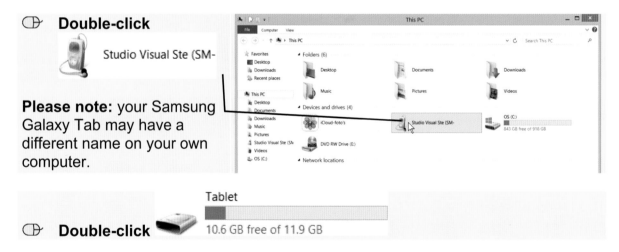

◯ **Double-click**

Studio Visual Ste (SM-

Please note: your Samsung Galaxy Tab may have a different name on your own computer.

Tablet

◯ **Double-click** 10.6 GB free of 11.9 GB

The photos and videos are stored in a folder called *DCIM*:

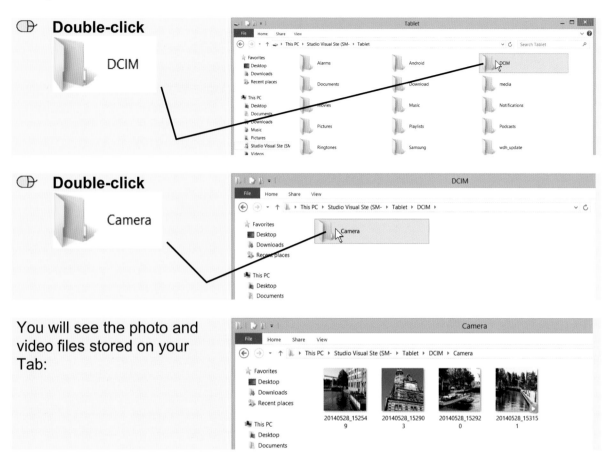

You will see the photo and video files stored on your Tab:

This is how you copy these photos to the (*My*) *Pictures* folder on your computer, for example:

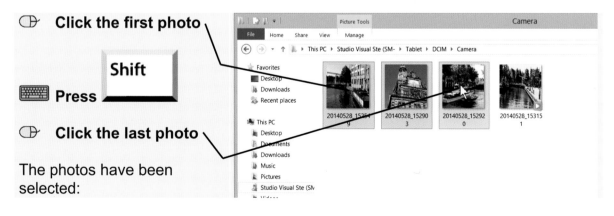

The photos have been selected:

When you drag the photos to a folder on your computer, they will be copied:

☞ **Drag the files to a folder, for example,** 📁 **Pictures**

When you see the message ➕ Copy to Pictures .

☞ **Release the mouse button**

Now the pictures have been copied to your computer. You can use the same method to copy a video to your computer.

💡 **Tip**

The other way round

This also works if you want to copy photos and videos from your computer to your Samsung Galaxy Tab. It is better to put the photos you copy in the 📁 Pictures folder. Then they will be displayed in a separate album. In the *Tips* at the end of this chapter you can read how to do this with *Samsung Kies 3*.

👉 **Close *Windows Explorer*** 👣⁸

👉 **Disconnect the Samsung Galaxy Tab from the computer**

7.7 Play a Recorded Video

In *section 7.2 Filming* you recorded a short video. You can watch this video with the *Video* app:

👉 **If necessary, tap** ⊞

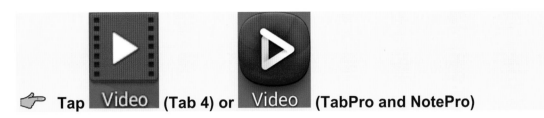

☞ **Tap** Video **(Tab 4) or** Video **(TabPro and NotePro)**

You will see the thumbnail image of the video you have recorded:

☞ **Tap the video**

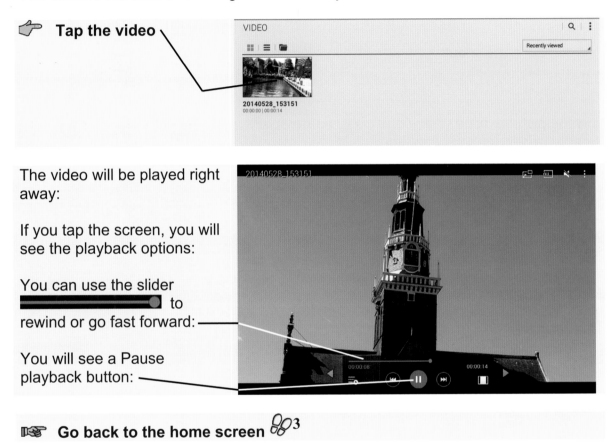

The video will be played right away:

If you tap the screen, you will see the playback options:

You can use the slider ▬▬▬▬▬▬● to rewind or go fast forward: ──────

You will see a Pause playback button: ──────

☞ **Go back to the home screen** 👣³

☞ **Lock or turn off the Samsung Galaxy Tab, if you wish** 👣¹⁴

In this chapter you have become acquainted with the *Camera, Gallery*, and *Video* apps.

7.8 Background Information

Dictionary

Album	The name of the folder that contains the photos you have taken with your Samsung Galaxy Tab, or the ones that have been stored on your Samsung Galaxy Tab, for example, by saving an attachment or saving a photo from a website.
Camera	An app with which you can take pictures and record videos. You can use both the front and rear cameras on the Samsung Galaxy Tab for this.
Gallery	An app that lets you view your photos on the Samsung Galaxy Tab.
Slideshow	An automatic display of a collection of images.
Video	An app with which you can watch the videos on your Samsung Galaxy Tab.
Zoom in	Take a closer look.
Zoom out	View from further away.

Source: User manual Samsung Galaxy Tab, Wikipedia

7.9 Tips

Tip
Use a photo as a background
You can also use your own photo as a background image for the lock screen or the home screen. You do that like this:

☞ **If necessary, tap the photo**

☞ **Tap** ⋮

☞ **Drag upwards over the menu**

☞ Tap **Set as**

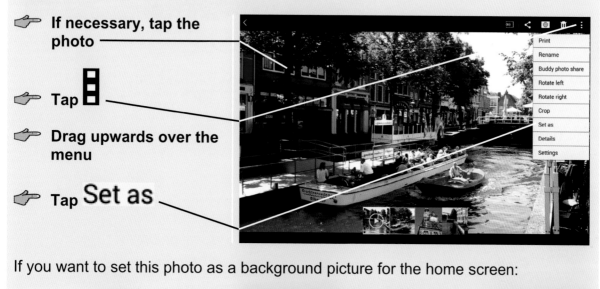

If you want to set this photo as a background picture for the home screen:

☞ Tap **Home screen**

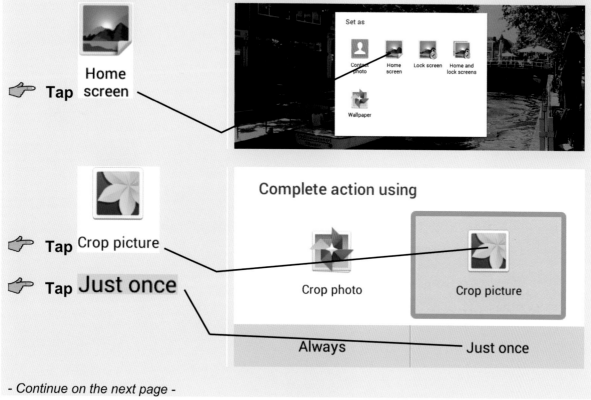

☞ Tap Crop picture

☞ Tap **Just once**

- Continue on the next page -

Select which part of the picture you want to use:

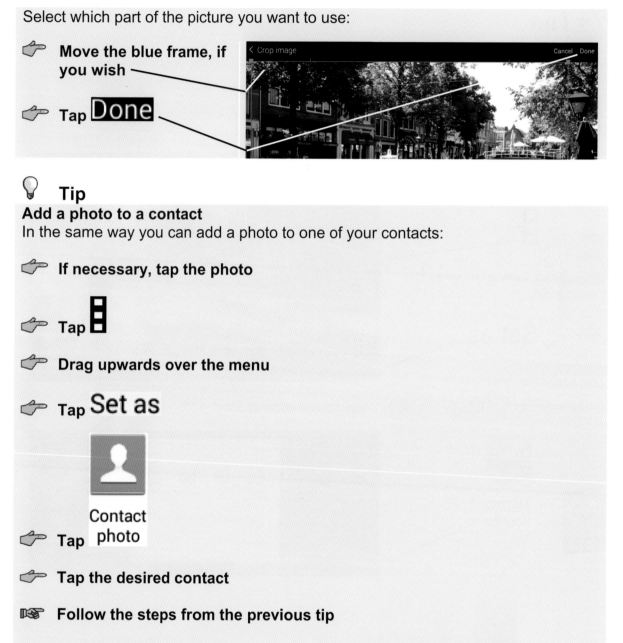

👉 **Move the blue frame, if you wish**

👉 **Tap** Done

💡 **Tip**

Add a photo to a contact

In the same way you can add a photo to one of your contacts:

👉 **If necessary, tap the photo**

👉 **Tap** ⋮

👉 **Drag upwards over the menu**

👉 **Tap** Set as

👉 **Tap** Contact photo

👉 **Tap the desired contact**

☞ **Follow the steps from the previous tip**

Now the photo has been added to the contact information for this person.

Tip

Photo editing
On the TabPro and the NotePro you can use simple photo editing tools in the *Gallery* app. For instance, rotating or cropping a photo, adjusting the color and exposure, and adding some effects. This is not available on the Tab 4. In the *Play Store* you can download various free and paid photo editing apps.

☞ **Open the *Gallery* app** 🦶23

☞ **Tap a photo**

☞ **Tap**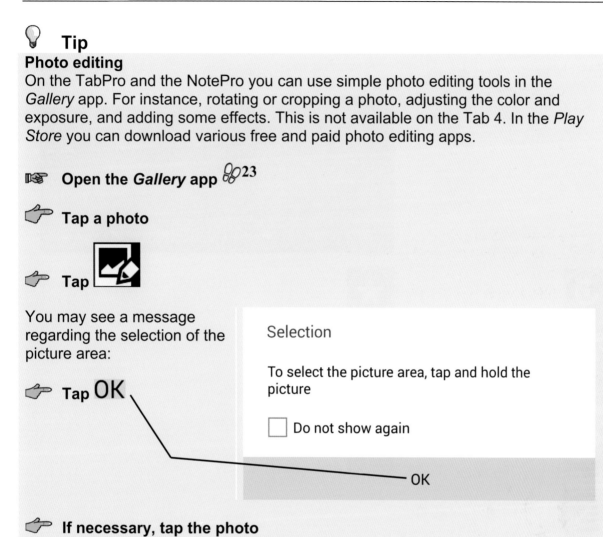

You may see a message regarding the selection of the picture area:

Selection

☞ **Tap OK**

To select the picture area, tap and hold the picture

☐ Do not show again

OK

☞ **If necessary, tap the photo**

- Continue on the next page -

Below the photo you will see several options. You can give some of these options a try:

Rotate **rotate a photo.**

Sticker **add a sticker.**

Crop **crop a photo.**

Drawing **draw on the photo.**

Color **adjust the color.**

Frame **add a frame.**

Effect **add an effect.**

You can undo any changes with ▨ :

Use **Save** to save the edited photo. The photo will be saved in the *Camera* album, in the *Gallery* app. The original photo will be saved as well.

⚪ Tip

Copy photos and videos to your computer with Samsung Kies 3
Previously, you have seen how you can use *Windows Explorer* to copy photos to your computer. You can also use *Samsung Kies 3* for this purpose:

☞ Open *Samsung Kies 3* 👣12

☞ Connect your Tab to the computer

☞ If necessary, close the help window 👣18

If you want to copy photos to your computer, you do the following:

By your Tab, click

🔲 Photos

You will see your photos:

If necessary, click

☰

Check the box ☑ by
the photos you want
to copy

Click 💾

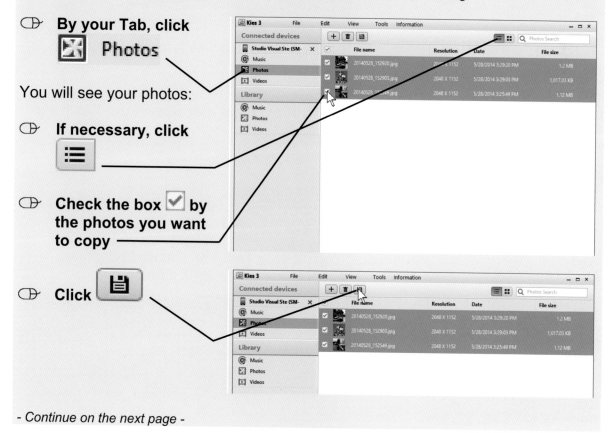

- Continue on the next page -

Select a location to save your photos:

☞ **If necessary, click**

▮ **Pictures**

☞ **Click**

┌─────────────────────┐
│   Select Folder   │
└─────────────────────┘

The photos will be copied to your computer. In the same way, you can copy your videos to the ▶ Videos folder.

☞ **Close the connection with *Samsung Kies 3* and disconnect the Tab from the computer** ✿¹³

💡 Tip

Copy photos and videos to your Samsung Galaxy Tab with Samsung Kies 3
Your Samsung Galaxy Tab comes in very handy if you want to show your favorite pictures and videos to others. You can also use some of the photos and videos stored on your computer and transfer them to your Tab. You can use *Windows Explorer* to do this, but you can also copy a folder with photos directly to your Samsung Galaxy Tab using *Samsung Kies 3*.

☞ **Open *Samsung Kies 3*** ✿¹²

☞ **Connect your Tab to the computer**

- Continue on the next page -

If you want to copy some photos, you do the following:

☞ **By your Tab, click**

⊞ Photos

☞ **If necessary, click**

≣

☞ **Click** **+**

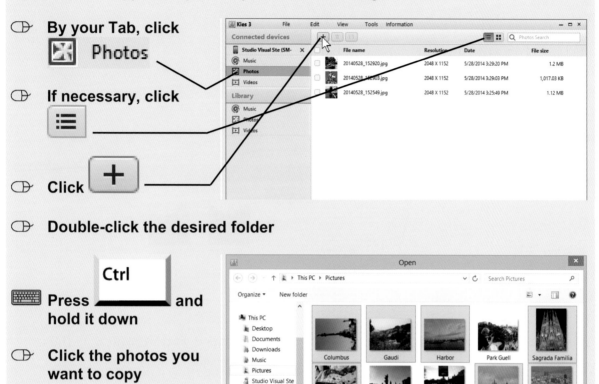

☞ **Double-click the desired folder**

⌨ **Press** **Ctrl** **and hold it down**

☞ **Click the photos you want to copy**

☞ **Click** **Open**

The photos will be copied to the *Camera* album on your Samsung Galaxy Tab. You can copy your videos in the same way.

☞ **Close the connection with *Samsung Kies 3* and disconnect the Samsung Galaxy Tab from the computer** ✂13

💡 Tip

Transfer photos from a memory card to the Tab

If you have a Micro SD card with photos, for example, you can transfer them to your Tab like this:

☞ **Insert the SD card into the memory card slot**

☞ **Open the *My Files* app** 👣²⁹

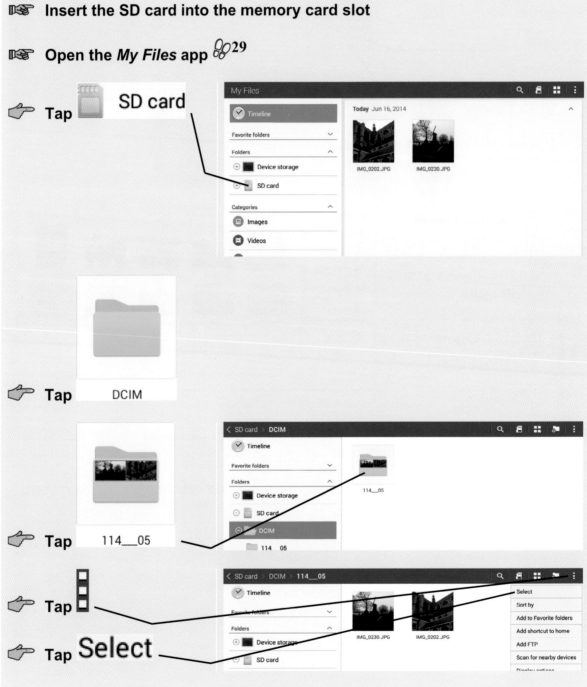

☞ Tap 📇 SD card

☞ Tap 📁 DCIM

☞ Tap 📁 114___05

☞ Tap ▫️

☞ Tap Select

- Continue on the next page -

Check the box ✓ **by the photos you want to copy**

Tap 📑

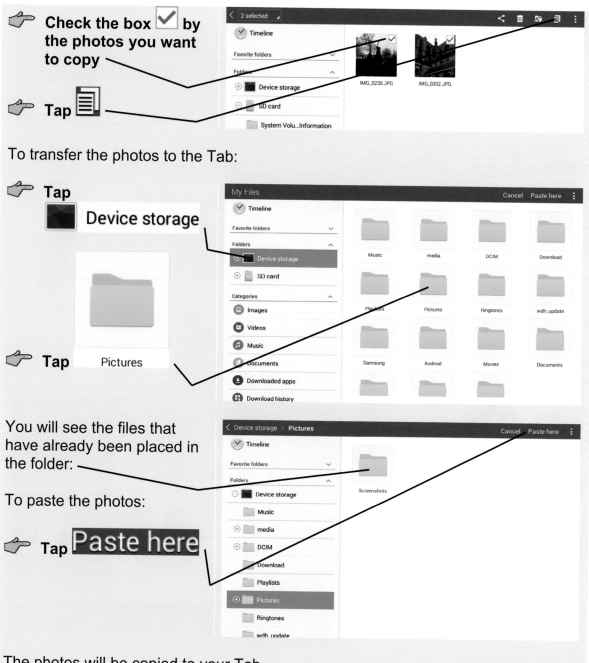

To transfer the photos to the Tab:

Tap

Device storage

Tap Pictures

You will see the files that have already been placed in the folder:

To paste the photos:

Tap Paste here

The photos will be copied to your Tab.

♀ Tip

Upload a video to YouTube
You can upload a video directly to *YouTube* from within the *Video* app. To do that:

☞ **Open the *Video* app** 👣²⁴

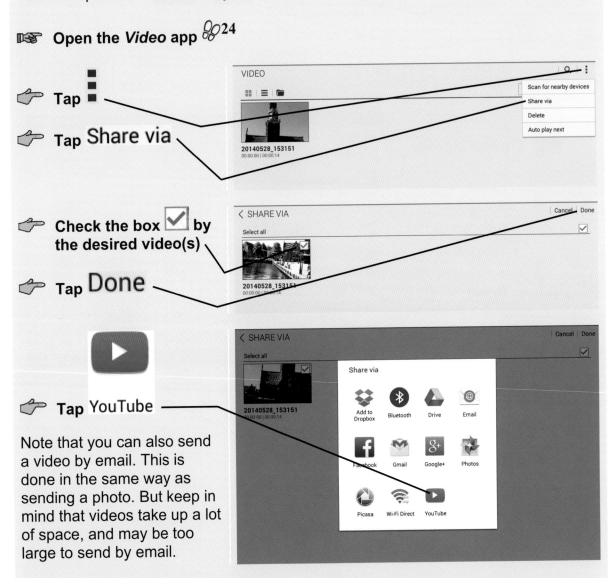

☞ **Tap ⋮**

☞ **Tap Share via**

☞ **Check the box ☑ by the desired video(s)**

☞ **Tap Done**

☞ **Tap YouTube**

Note that you can also send a video by email. This is done in the same way as sending a photo. But keep in mind that videos take up a lot of space, and may be too large to send by email.

In order to upload the video to *YouTube* you will need to sign in with your *Google* account. Next, you can enter the information for the video on the screen.

Tip!
YouTube also has its own app. This app is installed on your Tab by default. With this app you can easily watch all sorts of movies on *YouTube.* You can also create playlists with your favorite films, for example.

8. Music

Your Samsung Galaxy Tab comes with an extensive music player called the *Music* app. If you have music files stored on your computer, you can copy these files to your Samsung Galaxy Tab with *Samsung Kies 3*.

In this chapter you will learn how to:

- add music to the *Samsung Kies 3 Library*;
- copy music to your Samsung Galaxy Tab;
- play music on your Samsung Galaxy Tab;
- create a playlist on your Samsung Galaxy Tab;
- delete music from your Samsung Galaxy Tab.

Please note:

While you are using your Tab, you may see some screens that provide additional information about the operation of an app or the keyboard. You can read the information and tap Done or OK afterwards.

8.1 Adding Music to Samsung Kies 3

The *Music* app is the extensive music player that comes with your Samsung Galaxy Tab. If you have music files stored on your computer, you can copy them to your Samsung Galaxy Tab using *Samsung Kies 3*.

☞ **Open *Samsung Kies 3* on your computer** ✆**12**

You will see the *Samsung Kies 3* window. This is how you add a folder with music files to the *Library*:

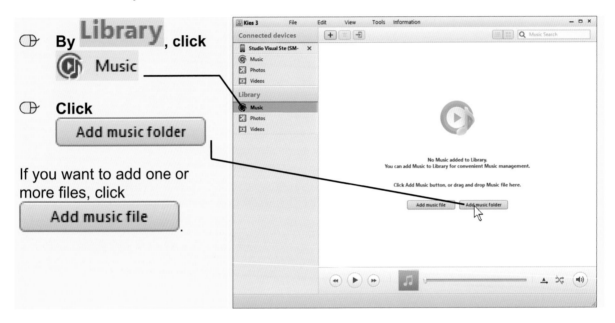

If you want to add one or more files, click

In this example we have chosen the *Windows Sample* folder. You can practice the following steps with the same folder or use one of your own folders with music:

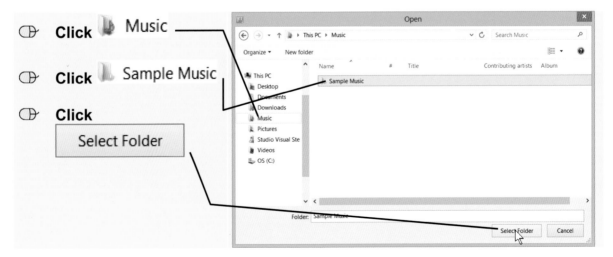

HELP! I see a window regarding the installation of a codec.

You may see a window regarding the installation of a codec. Codecs are necessary for playing music files.

Click Install

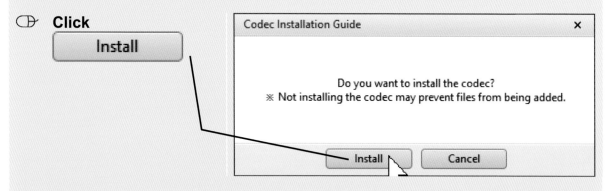

Your screen may turn dark and you will need to give permission to continue:

☞ **If necessary, give permission to continue**

You will be asked to agree to the license terms of the *MyFree CodecPack*:

Click I Agree

At the bottom of the window:

Click Next >

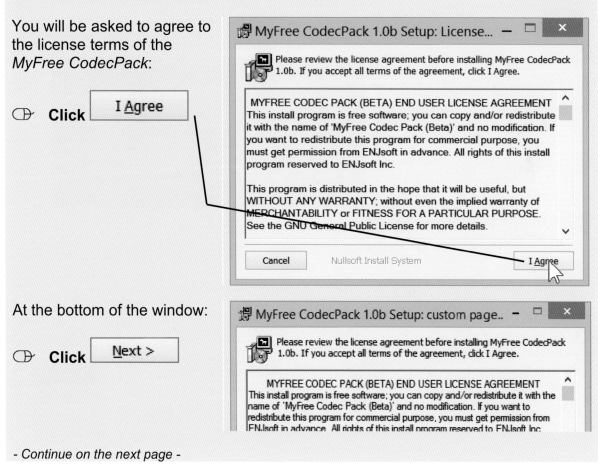

- Continue on the next page -

In the next window:

⊕ **Click** | Next > |

MyFree CodecPack 1.0b Setup: Installa... — ☐ ✕

Choose which features of MyFree CodecPack 1.0b you want to install.

Select components to install: ☑ MyFreeCodecPack 1.0 BETA

At the bottom of this window:

⊕ **Click** | Install |

MyFree CodecPack 1.0b Setup: Installa... — ☐ ✕

Choose the folder in which to install MyFree CodecPack 1.0b.

Destination Folder

C:\Program Files (x86)\MyFree Codec\1.0b beta   Browse...

Once the installation has finished:

⊕ **Click** | Close |

MyFree CodecPack 1.0b Setup: Compl... — ☐ ✕

Completed

Output folder: C:\Program Files (x86)\MyFree Codec\1.0b beta\XVID-CORE
Skipped: xvid.ax
Skipped: xvidcore.dll
Registering: C:\Program Files (x86)\MyFree Codec\1.0b beta\AC-3\ac3d...
Registering: C:\Program Files (x86)\MyFree Codec\1.0b beta\XVID-CORE...
Registering: C:\Program Files (x86)\MyFree Codec\1.0b beta\MyFree.ax
Create folder: C:\ProgramData\Microsoft\Windows\Start Menu\Programs...
Create shortcut: C:\ProgramData\Microsoft\Windows\Start Menu\Progra...
Created uninstaller: C:\Program Files (x86)\MyFree Codec\1.0b beta\uni...
Completed

Cancel   Nullsoft Install System   < Back   Close

You may need to add the music file again in *Samsung Kies 3*.

After a few moments you will see the songs in *Samsung Kies 3*:

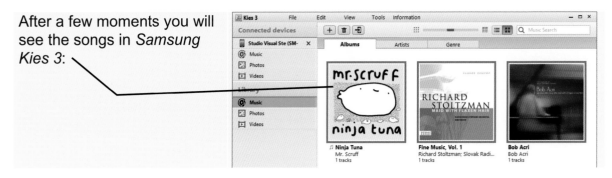

8.2 Copying Music to Your Samsung Galaxy Tab

Once the songs (also called tracks) are displayed in *Samsung Kies 3*, it is very easy to add them to your Tab.

☞ **Connect your Samsung Galaxy Tab to the computer**

☞ **If necessary, close the help window** ✂️18

The Samsung Galaxy Tab will appear in *Samsung Kies 3*. Select the tracks you want to copy:

⊕ **By** **Library**, **click**
   🎵 **Music**

⊕ **If necessary, click**
   ☰

⊕ **Click the first track**

⌨️ **Press** **Shift** **and hold it down**

⊕ **Click the third track**

⌨️ **Release** **Shift**

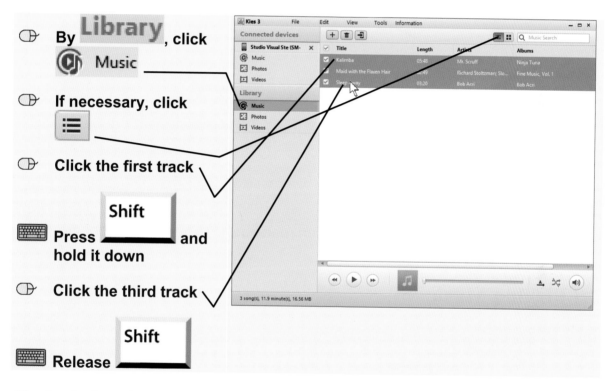

The tracks have been selected. Now you can copy them to your Samsung Galaxy Tab:

⊕ **Click** 📲

A blue bar in the lower right corner of the window indicates the copying is in progress:

View the content of the Samsung Galaxy Tab:

⊕ **By your Tab, click**

🎵 **Music**

You will see that the tracks have been transferred to your Tab: ——

Now you can disconnect the Tab and close *Samsung Kies 3*:

☞ **Close the connection with *Samsung Kies 3* and disconnect the Samsung Galaxy Tab** 🦶^{13}

☞ **Close *Samsung Kies 3*** 🦶^{7}

In the *Tips* at the end of this chapter you can read how to delete tracks from the Tab.

8.3 Playing Music

You can also use the *Music* app to play your music. To open the app:

☞ **If necessary, tap** ▦

☞ **Tap** Music **(Tab 4) or** Music **(TabPro and NotePro)**

👉 Tap Tracks

👉 **Tap a title, for example**

Sleep Away

MUSIC

| Playlists | Tracks | Albums | Artists | Folders |

Shuffle 4 tracks

K

Kalimba — Mr. Scruff — Ninja Tuna — 5:48

M

Maid with the Flaxen Hair — Richard Stoltzman/Slovak Ra... — Fine Music, Vol. 1 — 2:49

O

Over the horizon — Samsung — Samsung — 2:58

S

Sleep Away — Bob Acri — Bob Acri — 3:20

4 tracks

👉 **Tap the cover of the album**

MUSIC

| Playlists | Tracks | Albums | Artists | Folders |

Shuffle 4 tracks

K

Kalimba — Mr. Scruff — Ninja Tuna — 5:48

M

Maid with the Flaxen Hair — Richard Stoltzman/Slovak Ra... — Fine Music, Vol. 1 — 2:49

O

Over the horizon — Samsung — Samsung — 2:58

S

Sleep Away — Bob Acri — Bob Acri — 3:20

Sleep Away
Bob Acri / Bob Acri
0:01 — 3:20

The music player is displayed much larger:

You will see various buttons that can be used to control how the music is played:

Here is what these control buttons do:

 Mutes the volume.

 This button has multiple functions:
- tap once: go to the next song.
- press your finger on the button to fast forward.

 This button has multiple functions:
- tap once: go to the beginning of the current song.
- tap twice: go to the previous song.
- press your finger on the button to rewind.

Pause play.

Resume play.

 Drag the play button ⬤ or tap the bar to go to a specific part of the song.

Randomly play a song.

The songs will not be repeated.

Repeat:
- tap once: all songs will be repeated. The button turns into 🔁.

- tap twice: the current song is repeated. The button turns into 🔂.

 On the left-hand side of the screen you will see a pane with a list of all the tracks.

Add a song to the favorite tracks.

If you click 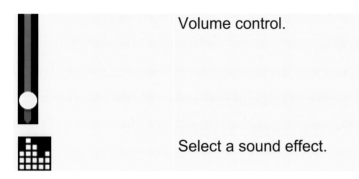, you will see more options:

Volume control.

Select a sound effect.

While playing a song, you can leave the *Music* app and do something else:

☞ Go back to the home screen ✌3

The music is still playing. You can display the control buttons of the *Music* app in the *Notification Panel* any time when using another app:

☞ Open the *Notification Panel* ✌1

You will see the volume control buttons of the *Music* app. To pause the music:

☞ **Tap** ⏸

☞ **Tap** ✕

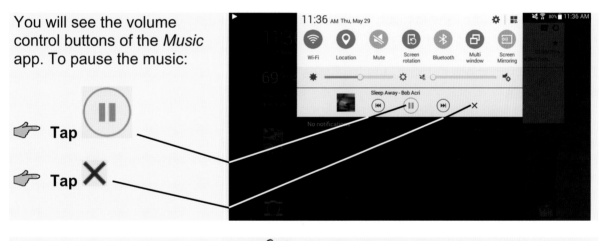

☞ Go back to the home screen ✌3

☞ Lock or turn off the Samsung Galaxy Tab, if you wish ✌14

You have nearly reached the end of this book. In this book you have learned how to work with the Samsung Galaxy Tab. Now you can start exploring some more and discover additional options and features this handy device has to offer.

8.4 Visual Steps Website and Newsletter

By now we hope you have noticed that the Visual Steps method is an excellent method for quickly and efficiently learning more about tablets, computers, other devices and software applications. All books published by Visual Steps use this same method.
In various series, we have published a large number of books on a wide variety of topics including *Windows*, *Mac OS X*, the iPad, iPhone, Samsung Galaxy Tab, Google Nexus tablet, Kindle, photo editing and many other topics.

On the **www.visualsteps.com** website you can click the Catalog page to find an overview of all the Visual Steps titles. Each title gives you an extensive description and allows you to preview the full table of contents and a sample chapter in PDF format. In this way, you can quickly determine if a specific title will meet your expectations.
All titles can be ordered online and are also available in bookstores in the USA, Canada, United Kingdom, Australia and New Zealand.
Furthermore, the website offers many extras, among other things:
- free computer guides and booklets (PDF files) covering all sorts of subjects;
- frequently asked questions and their answers;
- information on the free Computer Certificate that you can acquire at the certificate's website **www.ccforseniors.com**;
- a free email notification service: let's you know when a new book is published.

There is always more to learn. Visual Steps offers many other books on computer-related subjects. Each Visual Steps book has been written using the same step-by-step method with short, concise instructions and screen shots illustrating every step.

Would you like to be informed when a new Visual Steps title becomes available? Subscribe to the free Visual Steps newsletter (no strings attached) and you will receive this information in your inbox.
The Newsletter is sent approximately each month and includes information about
- the latest titles;
- supplemental information concerning titles previously released;
- new free computer booklets and guides;
- contests and questionnaires with which you can win prizes.
When you subscribe to our Newsletter you will have direct access to the free booklets on the **www.visualsteps.com/info_downloads** web page.

8.5 Background Information

Dictionary

Music	An app with which you can play music.
Playlist	A collection of songs, arranged in a certain order.
Samsung Kies 3	A program that lets you manage the content of the Samsung Galaxy Tab.

Source: User manual Samsung Galaxy Tab

8.6 Tips

 Tip

Create a playlist

One of the nice features in the *Music* app is the ability to create your own playlist. In a playlist, you collect your favorite songs and arrange them in the order you wish. Once you have done this, you can play the playlist over and over again. Here is how to create a new playlist in the *Music* app.

In the top left-hand corner of the screen:

☞ Tap Playlists

☞ Tap +

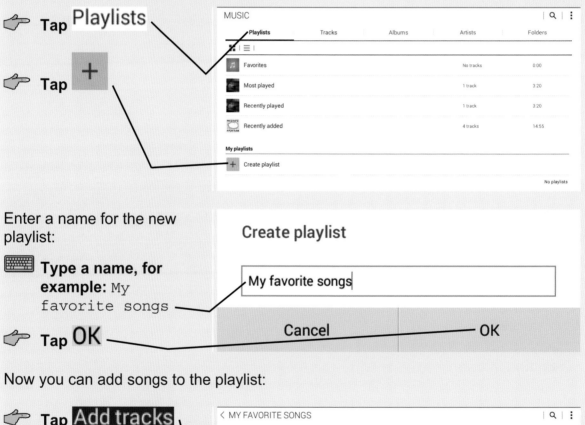

Enter a name for the new playlist:

⌨ **Type a name, for example:** My favorite songs

☞ Tap OK

Now you can add songs to the playlist:

☞ Tap Add tracks

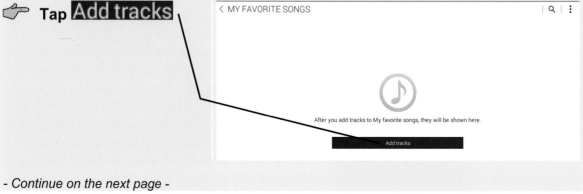

- Continue on the next page -

👉 **Tap the checkbox ✓ by the desired songs**

‹ 4 SELECTED			Cancel	Done
Tracks	Albums	Artists		Folders

☑ Select all

K

☑ Kalimba — Mr. Scruff — Ninja Tuna — 5.48

M

☑ Maid with the Flaxen Hair — Richard Stoltzman/Slovak Ra... — Fine Music, Vol. 1 — 2.49

O

☑ Over the horizon — Samsung — Samsung — 2.58

S

To remove a song from the playlist:

👉 **Tap the checkmark ✓ by the desired song to uncheck the box**

‹ 3 SELECTED			Cancel	Done
Tracks	Albums	Artists		Folders

☐ Select all

K

☑ Kalimba — Mr. Scruff — Ninja Tuna — 5.48

M

☑ Maid with the Flaxen Hair — Richard Stoltzman/Slovak Ra... — Fine Music, Vol. 1 — 2.49

O

☐ Over the horizon — Samsung — Samsung — 2.58

When your list is finished:

👉 **Tap** Done

If necessary, open the playlist:

👉 **If necessary, tap My favorite songs again**

MUSIC 🔍 ⋮

Playlists	Tracks	Albums	Artists	Folders

Favorites	No tracks	0:00
Most played	1 track	3:20
Recently played	1 track	3:20
Recently added	4 tracks	14:55

My playlists

My favorite songs	3 tracks	11.57
+ Create playlist		

You will see the new playlist:

If you tap **⋮**, you will see various options:

‹ MY FAVORITE SONGS + 🔍 ⋮

Shuffle 3 tracks 🔀

Kalimba	Mr. Scruff	Ninja Tuna
Maid with the Flaxen Hair	Richard Stoltzman/Slovak Ra...	Fine Music, Vol. 1
Sleep Away	Bob Acri	Bob Acri

Edit title
Change order
Via Bluetooth
Remove
Music square
Settings

Tip

Delete a track from the Samsung Galaxy Tab

In the *Music* app on your Samsung Galaxy Tab you can also delete songs. This is how you delete a song:

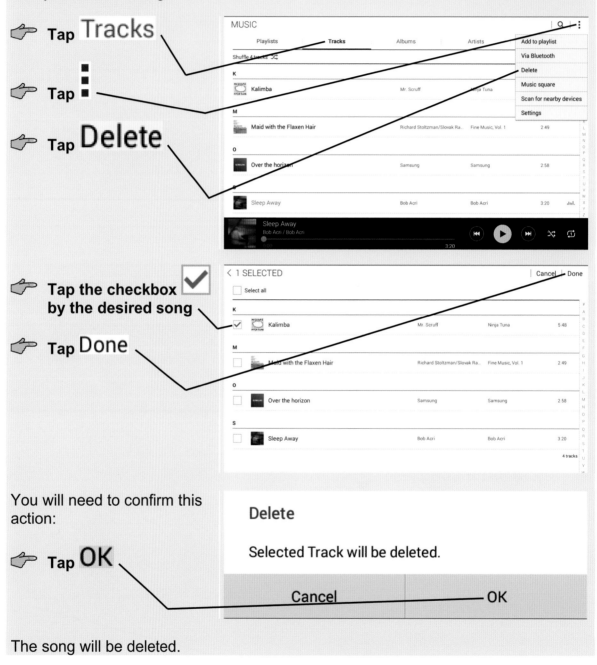

- Tap **Tracks**
- Tap **⋮**
- Tap **Delete**

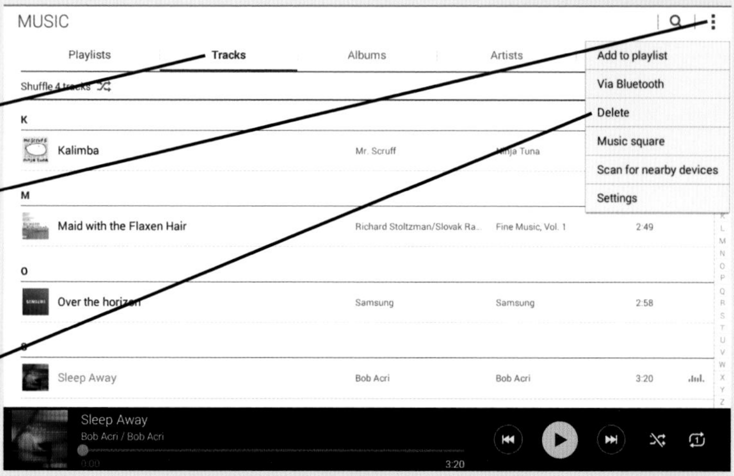

- Tap the checkbox by the desired song
- Tap **Done**

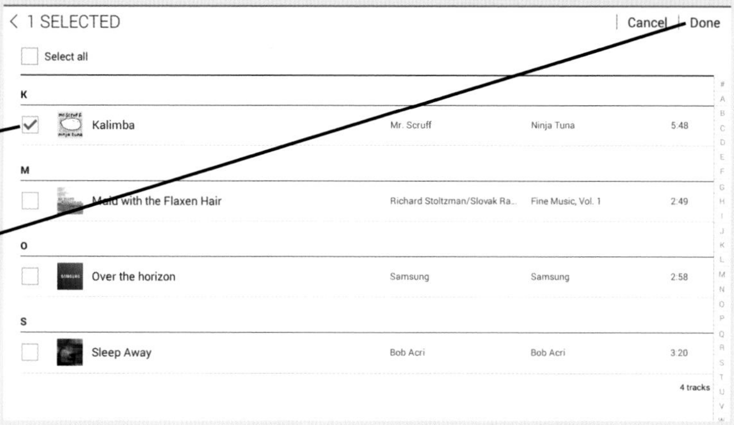

You will need to confirm this action:

- Tap **OK**

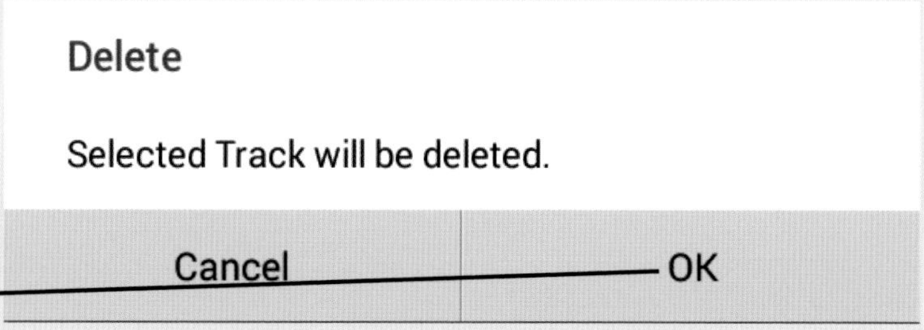

The song will be deleted.

Appendices

A. How Do I Do That Again?

The actions and exercises in this book are marked with footsteps: 🦶1
If you have forgotten how to do something, you can read how to do it again by finding the corresponding number in the list below.

🦶1 **Open *Notification Panel***
- Drag your finger downwards, starting at the top of the screen

🦶2 **Turn off Wi-Fi**
- Drag your finger downwards, starting at the top of the screen

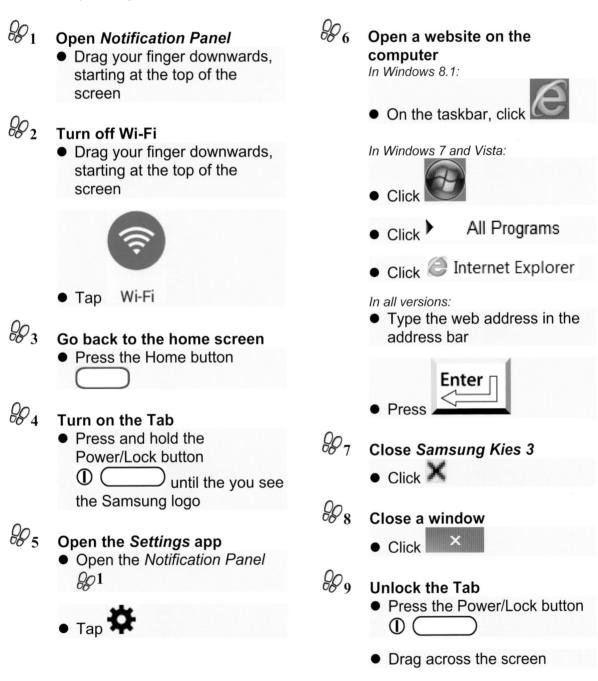

- Tap Wi-Fi

🦶3 **Go back to the home screen**
- Press the Home button

🦶4 **Turn on the Tab**
- Press and hold the Power/Lock button
  ⓵ ⬭ until the you see the Samsung logo

🦶5 **Open the *Settings* app**
- Open the *Notification Panel*
  🦶1

- Tap ⚙

🦶6 **Open a website on the computer**
In Windows 8.1:

- On the taskbar, click 🅔

In Windows 7 and Vista:

- Click 🪟

- Click ▶ All Programs

- Click 🅔 Internet Explorer

In all versions:
- Type the web address in the address bar

- Press Enter ↵

🦶7 **Close *Samsung Kies 3***
- Click ✖

🦶8 **Close a window**
- Click ✖

🦶9 **Unlock the Tab**
- Press the Power/Lock button
  ⓵ ⬭

- Drag across the screen

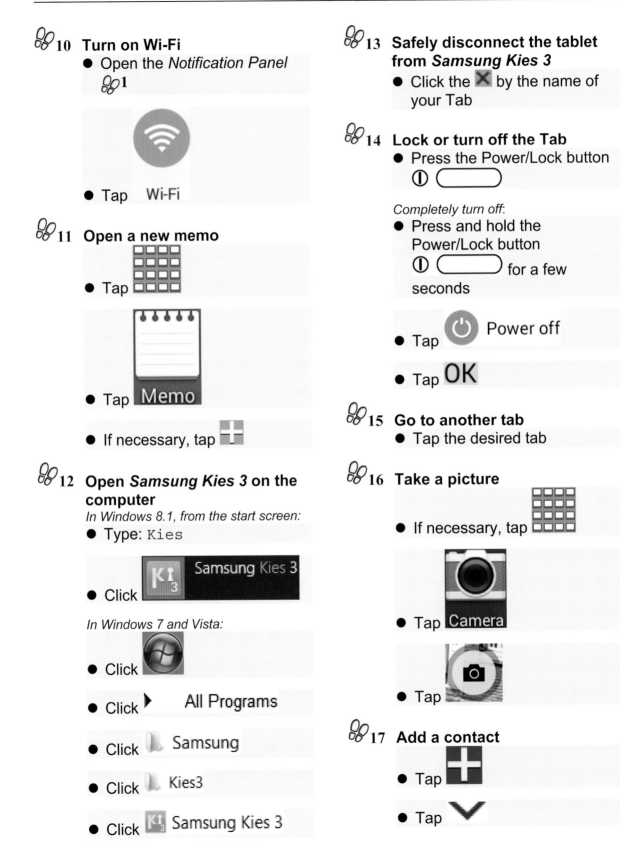

10 Turn on Wi-Fi
- Open the *Notification Panel*
  1
- Tap Wi-Fi

11 Open a new memo
- Tap
- Tap Memo
- If necessary, tap

12 Open *Samsung Kies 3* on the computer
In Windows 8.1, from the start screen:
- Type: Kies
- Click Samsung Kies 3

In Windows 7 and Vista:
- Click
- Click ▶ All Programs
- Click Samsung
- Click Kies3
- Click Samsung Kies 3

13 Safely disconnect the tablet from *Samsung Kies 3*
- Click the ✖ by the name of your Tab

14 Lock or turn off the Tab
- Press the Power/Lock button

Completely turn off:
- Press and hold the Power/Lock button for a few seconds
- Tap Power off
- Tap OK

15 Go to another tab
- Tap the desired tab

16 Take a picture
- If necessary, tap
- Tap Camera
- Tap

17 Add a contact
- Tap
- Tap ⌄

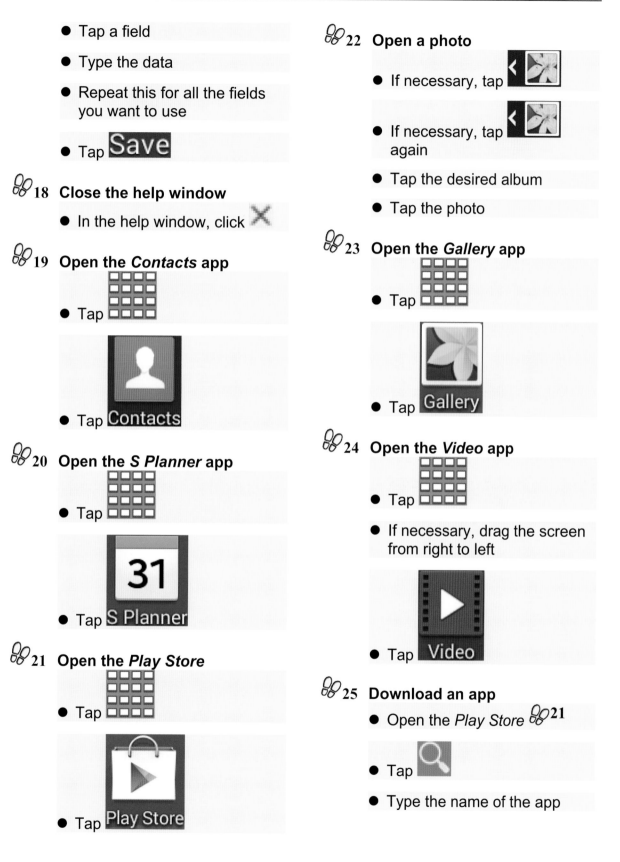

- Tap a field
- Type the data
- Repeat this for all the fields you want to use
- Tap **Save**

18 Close the help window

- In the help window, click ✕

19 Open the *Contacts* app

- Tap [apps grid]
- Tap **Contacts**

20 Open the *S Planner* app

- Tap [apps grid]
- Tap **S Planner**

21 Open the *Play Store*

- Tap [apps grid]
- Tap **Play Store**

22 Open a photo

- If necessary, tap [photo with arrow]
- If necessary, tap [photo with arrow] again
- Tap the desired album
- Tap the photo

23 Open the *Gallery* app

- Tap [apps grid]
- Tap **Gallery**

24 Open the *Video* app

- Tap [apps grid]
- If necessary, drag the screen from right to left
- Tap **Video**

25 Download an app

- Open the *Play Store* **21**
- Tap [search icon]
- Type the name of the app

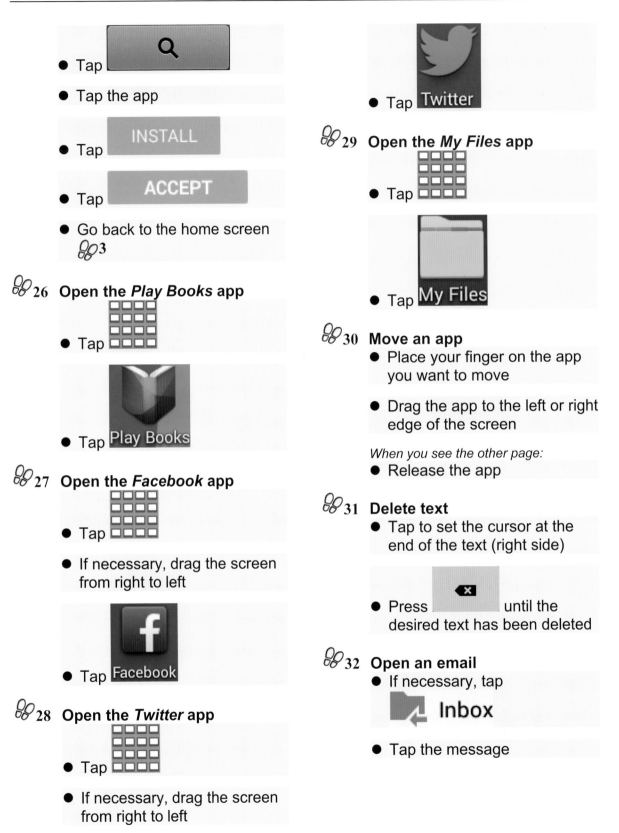

- Tap ⬜Q

- Tap the app

- Tap INSTALL

- Tap ACCEPT

- Go back to the home screen
  𝒫3

𝒫26 **Open the *Play Books* app**

- Tap ⬜⬜⬜⬜

- Tap Play Books

𝒫27 **Open the *Facebook* app**

- Tap ⬜⬜⬜⬜

- If necessary, drag the screen from right to left

- Tap Facebook

𝒫28 **Open the *Twitter* app**

- Tap ⬜⬜⬜⬜

- If necessary, drag the screen from right to left

- Tap Twitter

𝒫29 **Open the *My Files* app**

- Tap ⬜⬜⬜⬜

- Tap My Files

𝒫30 **Move an app**
- Place your finger on the app you want to move

- Drag the app to the left or right edge of the screen

When you see the other page:
- Release the app

𝒫31 **Delete text**
- Tap to set the cursor at the end of the text (right side)

- Press ⬅✕ until the desired text has been deleted

𝒫32 **Open an email**
- If necessary, tap

  📁⬅ **Inbox**

- Tap the message

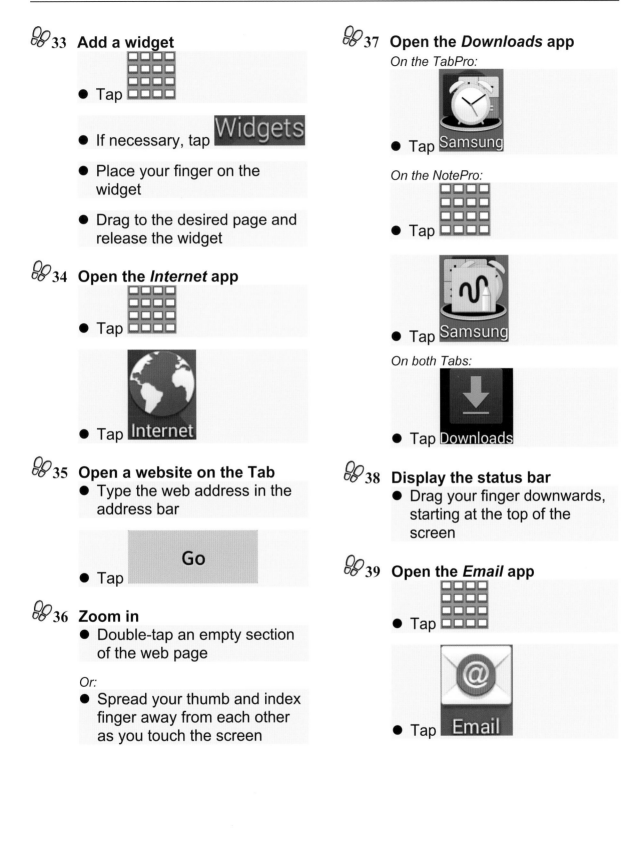

33 Add a widget

- Tap ▦

- If necessary, tap **Widgets**

- Place your finger on the widget

- Drag to the desired page and release the widget

34 Open the *Internet* app

- Tap ▦

- Tap **Internet**

35 Open a website on the Tab

- Type the web address in the address bar

- Tap **Go**

36 Zoom in

- Double-tap an empty section of the web page

Or:

- Spread your thumb and index finger away from each other as you touch the screen

37 Open the *Downloads* app

On the TabPro:

- Tap **Samsung**

On the NotePro:

- Tap ▦

- Tap **Samsung**

On both Tabs:

- Tap **Downloads**

38 Display the status bar

- Drag your finger downwards, starting at the top of the screen

39 Open the *Email* app

- Tap ▦

- Tap **Email**

B. Index

Digital Photo Editing with Picasa for SENIORS

Picasa, a very popular and free photo editing program, is one of the best choices for managing and editing your digital photos. In this book you will get acquainted step by step with some of the many things you can do with photos. You can sort and arrange your photos into albums. Edits can be applied manually or automatically. The contrast, color and exposure in a photo can be adjusted. It's possible to rotate photos, eliminate scratches or blemishes and remove red eyes. You can add effects or even text to a photo and create something unique to print or send. Picasa also gives you the option to make collages, view slideshows or create movies from your photos. A great way to share photos with family and friends!

> **GET ACQUAINTED WITH PICASA**

In this book you will work with practice photos. Once you have become familiar with the sorting and editing options available in Picasa you can start to work with your own photo collection. At the end of the book you will also learn how to import photos from a digital camera or other device to your computer. With Picasa and this book you will have everything you need to manage, edit and share your photos.

Author: Studio Visual Steps
ISBN 978 90 5905 368 7
Book type: Paperback, full color
Nr of pages: 272 pages
Accompanying website:
www.visualsteps.com/picasaseniors

Full color!

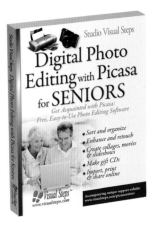

Learn how to:
- Sort and organize photos into albums
- Enhance and retouch photos
- Create collages and make gift CDs
- Create movies and slideshows
- Print and share photos online
- Import photos

Suitable for:
Windows 8.1, 7 and Vista

Windows 8.1 for SENIORS

*GET STARTED
QUICKLY WITH
WINDOWS 8.1*

The computer book *Windows 8.1 for SENIORS* is a great computer book for senior citizens who want to get started using computers. The book walks you through the basics of the operating system Windows 8.1 in an easy step-by-step manner. Use this learn-as-you-go book right alongside your computer as you perform the tasks laid out in each chapter. Learn how to use the computer and the mouse and write letters. This book also teaches you how to surf the Internet and send and receive e-mails. Be amazed at how fast you will start having fun with your computer with the new skills and information you will gain!

Author: Studio Visual Steps
ISBN 978 90 5905 118 8
Book type: Paperback, full color
Nr of pages: 368 pages
Accompanying website:
www.visualsteps.com/windows8

Full color!

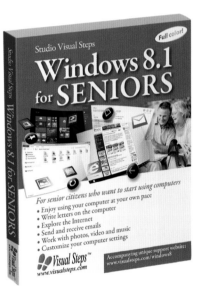

Learn how to:
- Become comfortable and enjoy using your computer
- Write letters and memos on the computer
- Send and receive messages by e-mail
- Explore the World Wide Web
- Customize your computer settings

Suitable for:
Windows 8.1 on a desktop or laptop computer

Mac OS X Mavericks for SENIORS

The Macintosh line of desktop computers and laptops from Apple has enjoyed enormous popularity in recent years amongst a steadily growing group of users. Have to Apple's user-friendly operating system but are still unsure how to perform basic tasks? This book will show you step by step how to work with Mac Mavericks.

> **LEARN STEP BY STEP HOW TO WORK WITH MAC OS X MAVERICKS**

You will learn how to use basic features, such as accessing the Internet, using email and organizing files and folders in Finder. You will also get acquainted with some of the handy tools and apps included in Mac Mavericks that makes it easy to work with photos, video and music. Finally, you will learn how to set preferences to make it even easier to work on your Mac and learn how to change the look and feel of the interface. This practical book, written using the well-known step-by-step method from Visual Steps, is all you need to feel comfortable with your Mac!

Author: Studio Visual Steps
ISBN 978 90 5905 090 7
Book type: Paperback, full color
Nr of pages: 296 pages
Accompanying website:
www.visualsteps.com/ macmavericks

Learn how to:

- Perform basic tasks in Mac OS X Mavericks
- Use Internet and email
- Work with files and folders in Finder
- Work with photos, videos and music
- Set preferences
- Download and use apps

Suitable for:

Mac OS X Mavericks on an iMac or Macbook

Word 2013 and 2010 for SENIORS

Microsoft Word is a popular and user-friendly word processing program. This book teaches you the basics of working with documents, from creating and editing documents to formatting text and working with styles and themes. You will also learn some of the

more advanced features such as working with an index and merging documents. This fully illustrated book features step-by-step instructions that will let you learn Word at your own pace. This is a practical book for the office, school or home!

Please note: In order to work with this book, you need to own Word 2013 or Word 2010 and have it already installed on your computer or have a subscription to Office 365, the online version.

Author: Studio Visual Steps
ISBN 978 90 5905 110 2
Book type: Paperback, full color
Nr of pages: 312 pages
Accompanying website:
www.visualsteps.com/word2013

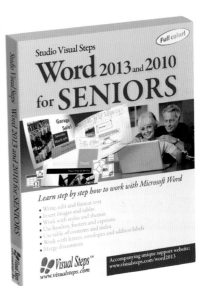

Learn how to:
- Write, edit and format text
- Insert images and tables
- Work with styles and themes
- Add headers, footers and captions
- Add a table of contents and an index
- Work with letters, envelopes and address labels
- Merge documents

Suitable for:
Microsoft Word 2013 and Word 2010
Windows 8.1, 7 and Vista

Prior experience:
Basic computer skills